Sea Survival

The Boatman's Emergency Manual

Robb Huff and Michael Farley

VK
1259
.H83
1989

FIRST EDITION
FIRST PRINTING

Copyright © 1989 by TAB BOOKS Inc.
Printed in the United States of America

Library of Congress Cataloging in Publication Data

Huff, Robb.
    Sea survival : the boatman's emergency manual / by Robb Huff and Michael Farley.
        p.   cm.
    Includes index.
    ISBN 0-8306-3077-7 (pbk.)
    1. Survival (after airplane accidents, shipwrecks, etc.)-
-Handbooks, manuals, etc. 2. Boats and boating—Safety measures-
-Handbooks, manuals, etc.   I. Farley, Michael B.   II. Title.
VK1259.H83   1989
623.88'8—dc19   88-32317
                                                   CIP

TAB BOOKS Inc. offers software for sale. For information and a catalog, please contact TAB Software Department, Blue Ridge Summit, PA 17294-0850.

Questions regarding the content of this book should be addressed to:

    Reader Inquiry Branch
    TAB BOOKS Inc.
    Blue Ridge Summit, PA 17294-0214

Edited by Eileen P. Baylus

Contents

Introduction

HISTORY IS REPLETE WITH TALES OF MARI-
time disasters. The possibility of being stranded in a small
raft without food and water for days or even months is a
very frightening one. Yet for anyone venturing forth on
the ocean, the possibility is very real. Even though technological advances have greatly improved man's oceangoing
capabilities, remember the ocean is still an alien environment that has proven its vast superiority over man time
after time. Even the soundest ship afloat offers absolutely
no guarantee that it will be able to weather an ocean
storm.

The sad truth is that too many boat owners traveling
the seas are in danger. Each year countless fatalities occur
at sea and on inland waterways. Hundreds of emergency
situations turn critical because mariners are, in most
cases, ill equipped and unprepared. Every mariner clearly
has a responsibility to himself and his crew to mentally and
physically prepare for the possibility of facing an ocean-
survival situation. Acknowledging the importance of this
responsibility is quite literally the first step toward surviving such an ordeal. Survival planning, then, is vital.

Sea Survival: The Boatman's Emergency Manual is
not just another personal account of a survivor's dramatic
ordeal at sea. Rather it is a comprehensive reference
manual that thoroughly and completely addresses all
aspects of ocean survival, from the planning and provisioning stages right through to the actual skills required to

maximize the chances of surviving an emergency situation on the ocean.

Every conscientious mariner and boat owner, from the novice who has just purchased his first boat to the highly experienced seaman, will find this book to be a necessary planning guide and valuable reference tool for outfitting his boat. The purpose of the book is twofold: To thoroughly prepare the mariner and aid him in equipping his boat with survival provisions before he leaves the dock, and to provide the mariner with a detailed reference source of basic survival skills vital to an actual ocean survival emergency.

The material is organized and presented in an easy-to-follow format, with useful illustrations, charts, and photographs. There are ample recommendations for provisioning boats with survival equipment, including pertinent facts needed for purchasing life rafts. Also included are suggested lists for purchasing provisions.

This book will familiarize the reader with the various types of signaling equipment available, as well as the actual operation and use of them in the field situation. Weather information pertinent to survival usage, such as assessing oncoming weather and identifying cloud types, is included. Basic survival skills, such as navigating the ocean, knowing abandon-ship procedures, signaling, effecting a land fall, living in a life raft, catching and storing fresh water, and distinguishing edible sea life, are all covered in detail. The emphasis of the survival skills is on use in the field situations, outlining steps, procedures and guidelines, rather than lengthy narratives. Finally, the yachtsman will have at hand practical information to aid him in dealing with common medical emergencies and preventing and treating dehydration and hypothermia. The psychological aspects of surviving a traumatic ordeal are also addressed, with techniques outlined for dealing with the depression, shock, and low morale that can seriously threaten the castaway's chance of survival.

This book will prove a valuable tool for the conscientious yachtsman—a tool that ultimately could mean the difference between life and death when coping with an unexpected disaster at sea. The necessity for survival planning when dealing with the unpredictable nature of the ocean environment certainly cannot be overemphasized.

Acknowledgments

THE AUTHORS WOULD LIKE TO EXTEND THEIR sincere gratitude to their wives, Lauren K. Farley and C. W. Huff. They initiated the first stages of this project. Lauren Farley's editorial skills were an invaluable asset, and C. W. Huff's persistence saw this manuscript through its final draft and on to the publisher's desk. C. W. Huff is an award-winning columnist.

We'd also like to acknowledge the following for their consideration and expertise: Avon Inflatables Limited; Dr. Daryl Davies; Ken Frazier, Santa Barbara Boat Works; Guest Co. Inc.; Betsy Huff; Peter Isler, Dennis Connor Sports, Inc.; Kilgore Corporation; Donald A. Meier, U.S.C.G., retired; Givens Buoy Life Raft; Olin Corporation; Capt. Richard Koskella, USAF; NOAA; Kelsey Burr, Survival Technologies Group; Mustang Manufacturing; Robert Tearnan, University of Hilo; Frank Torrance, Binnacle Yacht Sales; Scripps Institute of Oceanography; Stearns Manufacturing Co.; Survival International Inc.; Richard Switlik of Switlik Parachute Co.; and Jeff Worsinger, TAB BOOKS.

1

About Life Rafts

A *LIFE RAFT* IS A LAST-RESORT SURVIVAL system designed to provide flotation and protection from the elements, as well as to provide a platform from which to conduct survival efforts. Life rafts play a crucial role for survival in ocean emergencies. That is why any decisions you make concerning your life raft system might have serious and far-reaching consequences in an actual emergency. Therefore, before purchasing a life raft for your yacht, familiarize yourself thoroughly with the "whys and hows" of the basic construction and usage of life rafts.

The following section will focus on important points concerning purchase of a life raft, and routine maintenance and care of the life raft system. Although every yachtsman hopes that he will never need to deploy his life raft, he must also bear in mind that if and when the time does come, his life and the lives of his crew most likely will be affected by the integrity of the life-raft system he has chosen.

PURCHASING A LIFE RAFT

The acquisition of a life raft represents a major expenditure for most yachtsmen. Generally speaking, life rafts are not cheap. They are built to rigid standards and must be able to withstand both long-term storage, as well as the wear and tear of an actual emergency survival situation.

Every aspect of your vessel contains some degree of compromise. Life rafts are no exception. Most often, the decision concerning what type of life raft to buy and how much to spend will be dictated by such factors as available storage space, the number of crew on board, the type of cruising involved, and most obviously the budget you can afford.

Some yachtsmen feel that a life raft is an accessory item, and therefore feel hesitant about making a large expenditure on an item that they might never use. A life raft, however, should be regarded as a necessity, and it is far better to balance the budget in other ways than to compromise the integrity of the safety system. The cost of a life raft is usually minimal compared to the total invest-ment of the boat and its relation to the safety and well-being of the family.

How to Purchase a Raft. Many financing institu-tions will include the extra cost of purchasing a life raft in the original financing of the vessel. A thorough investiga-tion of prices available from the manufacturers will give you a good idea of the reasonable market value for the particular raft you have in mind.

You might find it advantageous to "bargain buy" on the market place, but always scrutinize the product care-fully and keep in mind that the savings of a few hundred dollars by buying a "demonstrator" model or a second-hand raft could have catastrophic consequences if serious defects are present. Life rafts are just that: life-saving instruments! Just as you would not expose an expensive sextant to unnecessary handling, neither would you want to have your survival system compromised.

Choosing a Raft. The next decision pertains to the size and design of the raft. (Figs. 1-1 through 1-4). Ideally, the size of the raft should be determined by the maximum

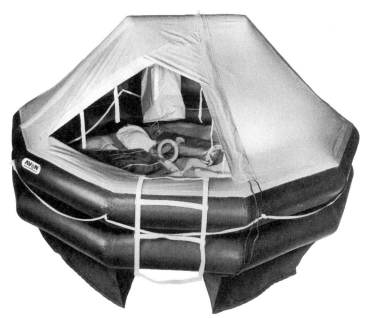

Fig. 1-1 One type of life raft. (Photo courtesy AVON INFLATABLES)

passenger capacity of the vessel. For instance, if the vessel has ten berths, then the life raft should accommodate ten people. Many yachtsmen, however, choose a more practical approach by purchasing a raft with a carrying capacity equal to the number of crew that is regularly on board.

Ultimately, the decision is left to the captain of the vessel. You might want to allow an additional margin of safety and comfort by purchasing a slightly larger raft or even an extra raft.

Choose a life raft that is sufficient for your needs, but that is still small enough and accessible enough to be launched under even the most adverse conditions. Remember, you might need to launch the raft in heavy seas or stormy weather, at night without lights, or while sinking or capsizing. Even the weakest crew member must be educated and drilled in launching and using the life raft before an emergency arises.

Fig. 1-2 Life raft. (Photo courtesy GIVENS BUOY LIFE RAFT)

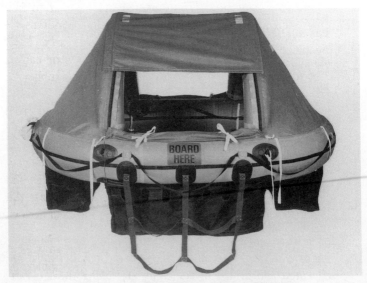

Fig. 1-3 Life raft. (Photo courtesy SWITLIK)

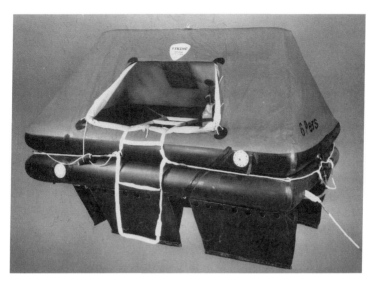

Fig. 1-4 Life raft. (Photo courtesy VIKING LIFE-SAVING EQUIPMENT)

Life Raft Construction. The manufacturers of modern life rafts are experts in the field and are constantly improving their products to include the most up-to-date materials and procedures. The construction material of a raft is a crucial element in its overall integrity. Most modern life rafts are made of a sturdy nylon or canvas fabric with a waterproof coating of neoprene rubber or Hypalon.

Survival Stores. Most life rafts purchased from manufacturers or their distributors will include a basic supply of "survival stores," which might vary according to the price of the raft and manufacturer. You should acquaint yourself with the wide range of safety devices and survival supplies available to make sure that at least the very basic and most necessary items are included in your life raft.

If you are not satisfied with what has been provided in your life raft, it is up to you to add any other supplies or devices that will enhance your safety and improve your chances of survival in an emergency.

Basic Items and Options. There is, of course, a gray area of opinion as to what is considered an absolute necessity on a life raft and what is not. Geographical factors also might play a role. Following is a concise list of those items generally considered to be fundamental to a life raft. (Fig. 1-5).

Flotation Capability. The raft must be able to stay afloat in adverse conditions while carrying the prescribed number of persons. It should be able to support over two-thirds its rated capacity with the largest buoyancy chamber completely deflated.

Automatic CO_2 Inflation System. The raft should include an automatic carbon dioxide inflation system that allows for unattended automatic inflation of the buoyancy chambers.

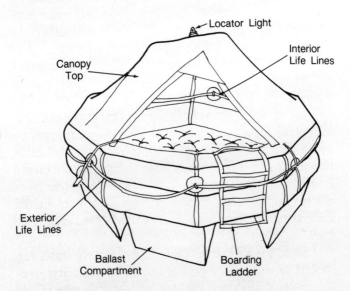

Fig. 1-5 Standard features of a typical survival life raft.

Manual inflation. Each buoyancy chamber of the raft should have a manual inflation mouthpiece, to allow for a carbon dioxide system failure and to inflate the raft at a later period. A hand pump or bellows should also be included.

Separate Buoyancy Chambers. For maximum safety, the raft should have at least two separate buoyancy chambers rather than an "all connected" single chamber, in the event that one chamber is punctured.

Canopy. The raft should have a canopy that is either automatically inflating or can be set up manually. It must be strong enough to withstand heavy winds or seas. A canopy of bright orange or yellow is best because these colors are highly visible. The canopy not only protects the life raft occupants from the elements, but can also maintain a safe temperature inside, can act as a sail, and can keep the occupants from falling overboard in heavy seas.

Double Floor. The raft should have a double floor of durable construction because exposure to cold ocean temperatures through a single floor can result in hypothermia. In addition to influencing temperature and comfort, a double floor also acts as an additional safeguard against possible rupturing from bumping into flotsam or marine animals.

If you already own, or intend to purchase a raft that has only a single floor, you can modify your raft to provide double floor protection. To do so, use heavy duty inflatable sleeping mattresses, or something similar that will create a "dead air" space between yourself and the bottom layer of the raft. Remember, however, that because of limited space this extra floor usually cannot be packed in the raft itself.

Stabilizing Pockets. The raft should have stabilizing pockets or some other type of stabilizing capability. Usually these pockets are attached to the underside of the inflatable raft. They provide added stability in the form of ballast by filling with water when the raft is deployed. (Note the different ballast designs in Figs. 1-1 through 1-4).

Colors. The raft should be designed with bright colors clearly visible on the top for aid in detection. Usually, the best distress colors are yellow or orange. (Note: On the bottom of the raft, however, bright colors are not advisable. It has been reported that a dark bottom will be of less interest or attraction to sea animals known to occasionally bump and rub the bottom of the raft. This bumping and rubbing can cause discomfort and possibly rupture the raft.) Furthermore, some manufacturers are designing the interior of the raft with less obtrusive colors to aid in reducing the effects of seasickness.

Sea Anchor. At least one sea anchor (and preferably two or even three) with the proper operating gear should be included in your life raft equipment. A sea anchor is used to create drag, reduce the chance of capsizing, and enable the raft to maintain directional stability.

Survival Kits. Some type of survival kit or kits should be a standard part of your life raft equipment. You can use the kit supplied by the manufacturer or any other kits that you might want to provision yourself (i.e., medical, repair, signaling, fishing, navigation).

Sea-activated Light. A seawater- or gravity-activated light on the exterior and interior top of the life raft is advantageous for finding and boarding the raft when it is deployed at night.

Inside Bracing Lines. Sturdy, inside lines can be used for tying off supplies and bracing in rough conditions.

Optional Items. The fine line between what is necessary and what is not is a matter of opinion, or perspective. The following items are usually considered optional in most life rafts, even though sound arguments for their necessity could be demonstrated. You will have to consider each item yourself to decide just how desirable or necessary you would consider it in your particular situation.

Grab Handles. Grab handles spaced evenly around the exterior perimeter of the raft are a desirable feature. They are particularly useful for grabbing on to when the raft is being righted after capsizing.

Grommeted Line. A sturdy line threaded through grommets all the way around the exterior perimeter of the life raft is useful for boarding the raft, for holding on to when floating beside the raft, for effecting a landfall maneuver, as well as numerous other uses that might arise in survival situations.

Boarding Ladder. A boarding ladder might be standard equipment with some life rafts. It is provided as both a safety and comfort feature.

Blow off/Topping off Values. This type of valve enables you to add or release small quantities of air in the buoyance chambers. Regulation of this nature is sometimes necessary because of changes in the air volume of the raft, which can be caused by temperature changes or small leaks.

Metal D-Ring. Some type of sturdy connection for towing various items such as sea anchors, lines, or game is advantageous in a life raft.

Maintenance and Storage. Once you buy a life raft, you must properly store and maintain to ensure that it will be in top operating condition when needed. The raft was purchased to perform a vital function in an emergency situation, and it is in your best interest to see that the raft is properly maintained and stored. A raft that has been allowed to deteriorate through neglect will be of little use in an emergency.

Rarely will a dealer have available a "demonstrator" model of a life raft. It is, however, worth your while to try to attend one of the national Marine Product Exhibitions that are held annually. Here the various manufacturers display their products and offer an opportunity for you to view a model similar to yours. This will give you a good perspective of the size of your future life support system.

You should also take the time to inquire directly regarding service and maintenance (Figs. 1-6 through 1-8).

STOWING THE LIFE RAFT

The whole point of purchasing and provisioning the life raft can be quickly negated if the raft is stored in an inaccessible place on your boat. Finding a place to store your life raft where it is in the most accessible place for an emergency situation and at the same time is safe from theft is admittedly difficult, and might necessitate some compromise.

To have the raft accessible during an instant capsizing or sinking, it must be located on deck, somewhere out of

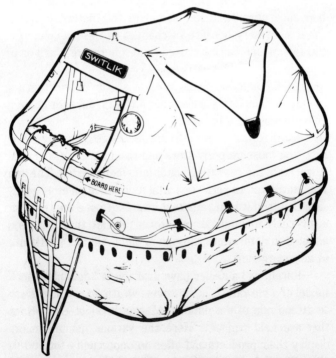

Fig. 1-6 U.S. Coast Guard Approved Life Raft. (Courtesy SWITLIK)

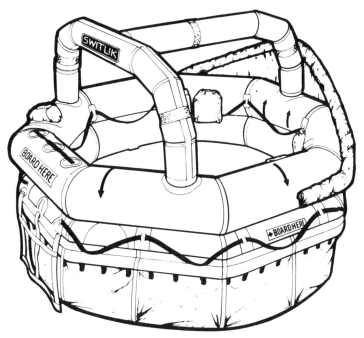

Fig. 1-7 Search and Rescue Life Raft. (Courtesy SWITLIK)

the way of rigging and working areas. Even though the deck is a vulnerable location in terms of theft or curious people, the majority of skippers seem to agree that it is the preferred location (Fig. 1-9).

The problem with storing the raft below deck while in port is that, although the intentions are good, it is too easy to put aside the chore of repositioning the raft on deck when you are going for a short sail.

How long would you need to locate your raft and launch it? Boats have been known to capsize and sink in minutes. And many an afternoon sailor has been caught in unforeseen storms with disastrous results.

The carbon dioxide inflation system should be stored toward the deck, so it will be protected. The line attached to the raft must also include enough length to allow the

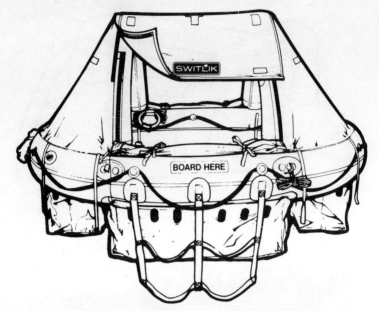

Fig. 1-8 Coastal Life Raft. (Courtesy SWITLIK)

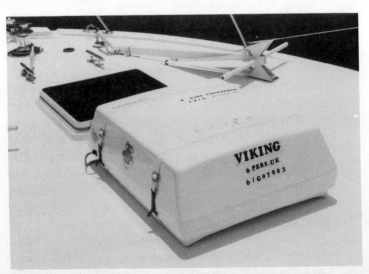

Fig. 1-9 Life raft in canister stowed on deck. (Photo courtesy VIKING LIFE-SAVING EQUIPMENT.)

raft to drift clear of the boat once it has been launched. But this line should not be cut prematurely, since the possibility of the raft drifting away from the boat before you have boarded it is especially high in a storm or high wind condition. (Follow the manufacturer's instructions concerning deployment of your life raft.)

Additionally, a knife should be sheathed and taped either to or near the raft container to ensure that in an emergency the person launching the raft can cut free the storage lines.

Usage

Detailed information concerning use of your survival equipment should be provided by the manufacturer. Study and understand these specifications before you need to use them. Familiarize yourself thoroughly with the operation of each piece of equipment that you own.

REPAIRS AT SEA

Generally, the areas of greatest strain will be the first to show signs of wear and will require greater attention. These areas include:

- The points where any lines or shackles, towing fixtures, etc. are attached to the raft
- The area where the floor and the flotation tubes are joined
- Areas where any abrasion or chafing occurs
- Areas around valves and seams

The "monitoring" of any leaks or repaired areas should be included in your watch routine. Remember that while a tiny leak must be viewed as serious, it is no cause for panic. Be sure to maintain adequate pressure in the buoyancy chambers by regulating the air when necessary. This will minimize strain on the seams of the raft.

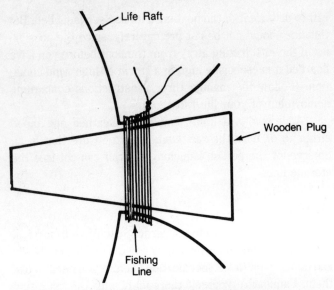

Fig. 1-10 A plug (of wood or other available materials) can be improvised to patch a life raft in case of a puncture.

Repairing a Major Leak

Take the following steps to repair a major leak in one of the chambers:

- Partially deflate the chamber.
- Use a proper patching kit and follow the directions supplied by the manufacturer. If you don't have a kit you will have to improvise with what ever materials and ingenuity you have available.
- Use a beveled wooden or plastic plug to patch major leaks. These plugs should be covered with some type of material before being inserted into the hole, and then bound with line to secure a better fitting (Fig. 1-10).
- Dry and then patch interior leaks. Exterior leaks (and areas of the floor) are more difficult to repair since the material will usually be wet.

2
Provisioning

THIS CHAPTER INCLUDES RECOMMENDED SUP-
plies and information to prepare you for an emergency.

FISHING KIT

Living off the sea can be easily accomplished with proper
preparation. The ocean is a perfect reservoir of food. Most
deep-sea fish are edible and provide sufficient nutrients to
sustain life.

A good fishing kit is easy to compile; most of the
items that you will need are small in size and low in price.
With the exception of a collapsible hand spear or gaff,
everything should fit into a small package. Quantities are
variable and will depend upon the size of your crew.

Hooks. You can never have too many hooks. Consid-
ering their size, 75 to 100 would not be too many. Include
several different sizes and shapes. Use caution in storing
hooks since a loose hook could damage the raft. Plastic
boxes that snap shut firmly are a good idea, as are empty
film cans since both are waterproof and will float.

Line. Include as much line as you can allow. The
average fish caught in a survival situation is much smaller

than you would think, so you must include light line, as well as heavy:

- 50 to 150 feet of 50-pound test monofilament
- 50 feet of both 15- and 25-pound test

Wire. Include a wire leader for large fish.

Weights. Include various sizes of weights. You might need a heavy weight to make the bait to sink rapidly past the smaller surface fish in search of the larger and deeper fish.

Knife. Include a sharpening stone for the knife.

Spear. A collapsible or folding 4-foot spear handle with detachable point is needed. Make sure to pack the spear head carefully.

A Metal Gaff Hook. You also will need a metal gaff hook. Please pack it carefully.

Book. A fish identification book for reference is handy to have.

RAFT REPAIR KIT

A repair kit usually will be provided by the manufacturer of the life raft. Inspect it to see that it is complete. Documented records of actual survival situations suggest that the following items, if not provided, should also be added:

- Patches (and scissors to cut for size and fit)
- Adhesive (extra supplies of epoxy resin and catalyst or a faster setting contact adhesive glue)
- Plastic or wooden threaded plugs for large holes in the raft
- Solar still repair kit and patches

CLOTHING

Space is the limiting factor for clothing provisions. Here are some suggestions:

Wool. Wool is a good choice of material because of its insulating qualities even when wet. Its ability to absorb perspiration makes it superior to cotton or down.

Synthetics. Available on the market today are various synthetic fibers that are effective and space saving. (They perform much better than down when wet.)

It is a good idea to pack a supply of clothes and store them in an accessible place so you can turn your attention to other things during the emergency situation.

WATER STORES

Deciding the quantity of emergency water stores to take along can be difficult. Medical authorities have established that a *minimum* of 1 pint of water per day is sufficient for one person. (However, 2 quarts of water per day is necessary for a person to exist without suffering any loss in efficiency.)

One method of ensuring that you'll have water with you is to tie three or four containers to the raft while it's stored on deck. Then, once the raft is deployed the containers will be attached and floating with the raft. (Watertight seals are necessary and plastic jugs must be stored out of the sun to avoid spoilage.) A gallon plastic container three-quarters full will float.

Another method of carrying water stores is by purchasing water already packaged in cans. Usually the provisions kit supplied by the manufacturer will include several of these cans. A can opener and a plastic top for resealing the can once it has been opened must be included.

Solar stills and desalinization kits are each a must in your emergency stores. Ideally, you should include more than one of each. The desalinization kits can be used when conditions restrict the use of a solar still.

Six packs or cases of beer, although nicely packaged, are not advisable in an emergency backup. Alcohol has absorbing qualities that can deplete vital body fluids, thus increasing the danger of dehydration.

NAVIGATIONAL EQUIPMENT

Navigation in a survival craft might not hasten your voyage to a certain landfall, but it most definitely can provide you with the knowledge on which to base vital decisions. Knowledge of position and progress are excellent morale boosters. Rationing schedules might be influenced by how successfully you determine your position.

The following gear, prepacked in a small container, will provide you with adequate equipment with which to ascertain an approximate position:

- Plastic sextant
- Nautical almanac
- H0249 sight reduction tables
- Watch
- World time zone chart
- Surface current chart of the world
- Universal plotting chart
- Navigation plotter
- Liquid compass
- Charts providing an overview of your intended cruising areas

ADDITIONAL PROVISIONS

Following is an extensive summary of optional survival items. These items are frequently included in emergency survival kits. Although every item should be included in the ideal survival kit, limiting factors of space and economics will necessitate compromises.

- Sea Anchors (two or three)

    Because nylon line will stretch, it is preferable to rope. Using it to connect the sea anchor to the raft will provide a buffer effect on the ocean's tug. This will lessen the wear and strain at the point of connection.

    Occasionally the sea-anchor line will unravel from continuous twisting. You can prevent this problem by installing a swivel shackle at the point where the line and anchor are connected.

- Flashlight (waterproof with spare batteries and bulb taped to it) Reverse one of the batteries inside the flashlight to guard against dead batteries should the light be inadvertently switched on.
- Large sponge
- Knife (one sheathed 6-inch single-edged blade and one or two other knives of different design)
- Knife sharpening stone
- Can openers (two or more)
- Pencils
- Small plastic sealable bags
- Graduated water bag
- Mending tape
- One space blanket per person
- 50 feet to 100 feet of ¼-inch nylon line
- Air bellows (check manufacturer's supply kit)
- Bailing container
- Rain catchment (plastic tarp or the equivalent)
- Sunglasses for each person
- Sunscreen
- Survival suit (for cold areas)
- Wet suit

SIGNALING PROVISIONS

There are several types of signaling devices that should be included in basic provisions, but opinions vary as to quantities. Research has shown that literally hours worth of signaling time might be required. For this reason, a supply of signaling devices that will last only 15 to 20 minutes might not be realistic.

The decision as to how much of each item to include will be influenced by available space, budget, and priority evaluations. Weigh decisions objectively and reach a balance that will fit your particular situation without compromising your safety. It is important to allow for both the malfunction and loss of vital equipment. In emergency situations this happens all too often.

Personal Safety Pack. You can wear a small "safety pack" on your belt while aboard your vessel. Unlike a life jacket, which is typically worn only during bad weather and on night watches, you should wear the safety pack at all times. The contents are greatly restricted by size, and mainly includes signals with "locating" capabilities for the man-overboard situation. It is usually equipped with the following:

- Plastic signal whistle
- Dye pack
- Signal mirror
- Small waterproof light (chemical light)

Personal Floatation Device Equipment. The following is a list of suggested signaling devices that can be secured by tape to each personal flotation device (PFD) for use in an emergency (Fig. 2-1):

- One orange smoke flare, daytime use
- One red night flare
- Plastic whistle (on lanyard near the head area and usable without having to untie it)
- Water activated light (preferably a strobe)
- Reflective tape, attached to the PFD around the neck and shoulder area
- A small, light, radio beacon

Life Raft. Signaling stores for a life raft should be capable of floating and have a quick fastening lanyard so they can be attached to the raft as quickly as possible in an emergency. Lanyards with snap shackles, for example, would be excellent to use. Also, a small and sturdy plastic box, if wrapped in plastic or sealed with duct tape, would be waterproof and possibly capable of floating.

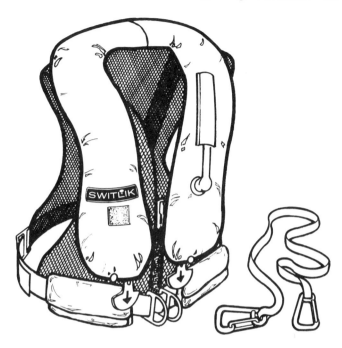

Fig. 2-1 One example of a PFD, Personal Flotation Device. (Illustration courtesy Switlik Fastnet Crew Vest.)

Following is a suggested list of signaling stores for a life raft (Quantities listed are recommended minimums and should be increased whenever conditions permit):

- 6 to 9 long-burning orange smoke flares
- 6 to 9 red night flares
- 6 to 8 bottles or packets of dye marker
- 2 signal mirrors on lanyards (at least one of metal construction)
- 2 plastic whistles with lanyards
- 1 aerial flare kit (preferably large-caliber pistol type) with a reasonable supply of flares for the kit)
- Emergency Position Indicator Radio Beacon (EPIRB) radio locator beacon

FOOD STORES

Obviously, any food that you can bring with you will be to your benefit. Most life-raft emergency kits contain only candy. The usual purpose for including candy in emergency rations is that sugar (and also carbohydrates) assimilate quickly in the body and hold up well under long-term storage. Candy requires less fluid to digest than does more nutritious foods high in protein.

Many authorities advise you not to eat any protein when there is a shortage of water because protein requires a considerable amount of body fluids for its assimilation and digestion. Remember, the control and preservation of your body fluids is crucial in conditions of heat and limited water supply.

A "grab bag" of normal food is a good idea, but you should update it periodically to ensure that it has not spoiled or merely powdered away. You could include cereals, sweets, evaporated milk, seeds for sprouting, or lemon juice in a plastic container. Seal them against moisture and make sure they will float.

Vitamins are another necessary item to include in your emergency rations. They take up minimal space and can provide you with the nutritional needs you will be lacking over the period of time afloat.

The prolonged deficiency of any vitamin can hinder the normal functions and abilities of the body. One of the most prevalent dangers in the survival situation will be the lack of Vitamin C. Vitamin C deficiency causes "scurvy." Maritime history is documented with accounts of scurvy, and it is still as much a threat today.

Fresh fruits supply us with most of our Vitamin C. Emergency stores are not able to provide such a luxury as fresh fruit, so a supplement must be taken along to ensure that this very important vitamin is included.

Considerable amounts of vitamins can be obtained from eating raw fish. Substantial levels of vitamins A and

D are present in the oils of many fish. Turtles also contain high levels of A and D. Fish, liver, and egg yolks will provide some of the B vitamins.

Dehydrated foods are not recommended for your survival rations pack. Their digestion requires far too much water to make them practical.

THE GRAB-BAG APPROACH

Preparing a grab bag (for food, clothing, medicines, or whatever) is probably the most effective way of equipping yourself for an emergency. Because space is a very limited and valuable commodity on a boat, the decision of what to pack is essential and will require some serious consideration (Fig. 2-2).

You also must decide what items will be stored and considered untouchable and what will be available for use on a daily basis. Food stores set aside for emergency

Fig. 2-2 Flotation grab bag for abandon ship supplies. (Courtesy Survival Technologies Group.)

situations, such as the grab bag, must not be tampered with or taken from for any reason.

A well-stocked medicine kit poses different problems. A kit designed for daily needs would be larger and more complete than a kit compiled exclusively for the life raft. For economic reasons, it would be difficult to provide a duplicate of every thing necessary for both the boat and the life raft. Weigh your decisions carefully, however, and attempt to reach a balance that will leave you as well prepared as possible.

MEDICAL KIT

Complete medical kits for boats are restricted by available space. Even more restrictions apply to the survival craft. The following section on medical supplies includes a reasonably extensive supply of ready-to-apply first aid and "final aid" items. It comprises what would be a basic "medical chest" for a boat.

The ship's "medical chest" should be taken into the survival raft. Remember, if your ship goes down in a matter of minutes, you might have only enough time to launch your raft. For this reason, pack a condensed and smaller medical kit that is off limits for normal use and stored with your basic survival supplies. You can draw from the following list if you choose to package a survival medical kit.

Note: There are no quantities or dosages included in the following list. Quantities will, of course, depend on the number of crew normally aboard; obtain dosages from your physician.

Supplies

- Large plastic syringe, for stomach pump and aspiration
- Waterproof adhesive tape, (as opposed to bandages or pins for securing)

- Adhesive tape bandages
- Cotton wool
- Gauze (sterile and individually packed)
- Petroleum jelly
- Bandage, both cotton and absorbent types
- Inflatable splints
- Razor blades, (one edge) sealed against moisture
- Scalpels, various sizes
- Artery foreceps
- Safety pins
- Scissors, 3-inch blades
- Hot water bottle with enema attachment and tube (stored elsewhere than the medical box)
- Snake-bite kit
- Tourniquet, ¾- to 1 inch wide
- Thermometer, clinical with case
- Sling, cloth or muslin
- Tweezers
- Hypodermic syringe and needles
- Butterfly strips and bandages
- Sponge, sterile
- Suture circle needle
- Knife
- Waterproof adhesive dressing, assorted sizes
- Wire saw, for cutting through bones
- Jaw spreader and bite stick
- Stethoscope
- Iodine swabs
- Triangular bandage
- Eye pads
- Lip balm
- Flashlight
- First-aid instruction booklet

Discuss the medical kit with your physician to tailor it to your personal needs and to obtain any controlled substances. The controlled substances in your medical chest are your responsibility and must be protected against loss or abuse. (It is, however, not advisable to ever have the kit locked.)

The medical kit container should be large enough to include most of the medications needed, but still compact enough to be realistic for storage and handling. A plastic fishing tackle box, preferably watertight is excellent for this purpose. It allows for compactibility, is corrosion proof, and provides assortment trays. Pack or sheath all pointed and sharp instruments to protect them from damaging the raft and from exposure to the elements (Fig. 2-3).

Medications

The following list recommends a minimum number of possible medications to include in your medical kit:

- Ampicillin: a potent broad-spectrum antibiotic used for severe respiratory or kidney infections accompanied by high fever

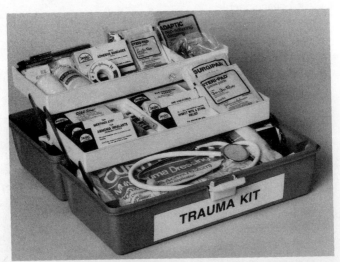

Fig. 2-3 Example of prepackaged medical kit. (Courtesy Marine First Aid, Healer Products Inc.)

- Gantrisin: for kidney and bladder infections
- Tetracycline: also a potent broad-spectrum antibiotic. Used as drug of first choice after penicillin for respiratory and skin infections
- Penicillin V.K.: the drug of first choice for respiratory infections, sore throats, and skin infections
- Procaine penicillin: injectable penicillin for infections that are fairly severe or for the patient who may be unable to hold down oral medicines because of vomiting
- Valium: an antianxiety drug also used for muscle relaxation. Will cause moderate to severe drowsiness
- Compazine: for prolonged vomiting (more than 24 hours)
- Empirin #3: pain medicine
- Morphine injection capsules
- Lomotil: antidiarrheal medicine
- diphenhydramine hydrochloride: an antihistamine. Used for itching from rashes
- Alcohol (rubbing or isopropyl)
- Analgesic ointment: i.e., Lanocain, Nupercainal
- Meat tenderizer: for jellyfish stings.
- Neosporin
- Soap, Phisohex
- Sunburn ointment, sun screen
- Zinc oxide
- Adrenalin
- Antiseptic cream
- Motion seasickness pills. Include suppository or transdermal (through the skin) types for use in the event a victim is too ill to ingest a pill
- Acetaminophen, nonasprin tablets
- White petroleum jelly
- Pepto-Bismol tablets
- Ammonia inhalants

3

All About Signals

MAN HAS DEVISED NUMEROUS AIDS TO HELP the isolated survivor stand out against the elements to increase his chances of being rescued. Each type of signaling device has a specific design and purpose, as well as definite operating limitations. The prepared mariner, to be effective in most situations, should have a wide range of signaling devices to allow him the greatest chance of rescue.

The object of any signaling action or device is to create a spectacle and call attention to yourself. In an actual distress situation there is no illegal method of doing this. Any method or device that will get you rescued is justifiable.

As of January 1, 1981, boats using American coastal waters or the Great Lakes are required by law to carry approved distress signals. Every boat 16 feet and over is required to carry approved day and night visual distress signals. (Boats under 16 feet are required to carry approved night signals between sunset and sunrise.) Although the offshore cruiser does not normally fall within these jurisdictions, common sense and safety dictates that the cruising yacht also should be provisioned with an adequate supply of distress signals (Fig 3-1).

SIGNALS

Marine distress signals can be categorized according to design and purpose: those that are used to alert, and those that are used to locate.

Being able to alert the rescue party of your situation or whereabouts is essential, since the chance of being spotted accidentally is minimal. Moreover, the ocean can be so effectively deceiving to the human eye, that you also need a location-type signal that will enable the rescue craft to find you or "home" in on your position.

The effect of heavy swells on the visibility of any floating object in the ocean is well understood by sailors. Any mariner who has approached an unlit landfall at night can testify to the hazards and perceptual difficulties. Consider the problem in a survival situation at sea: A rocket flare is sighted four miles off to port in the distance, in heavy seas, and at night. The chance of an alerted ship pinpointing and reaching the position of the raft is slim, unless the raft can provide a constant location signal or reference.

A well-prepared supply of signals must contain both alert and locate devices. Although some distress signals can function as both, each device will usually serve one purpose more effectively.

Alert Signals

There are no strict distinctions between what would qualify as an alert signal or what qualifies as a locate signal. Obviously, any device that successfully alerts rescue can be called an alert signal. There are, however, certain devices that lend themselves more readily to the alert purpose.

Fig. 3-1 Manufacturer's display of signaling devices available.
(Photo courtesy OLIN.)

Any signal that is capable of attaining great heights (such as a rocket flare) is far more useful for alerting the attention of distant ships than most other types of visual signals. Your sighting distance on the ocean will be affected by the following: the curvature of the earth, the distance between your signal and the viewer, and the height of your signal. It is important to understand how each of these factors influences the effectiveness of your signaling device (Fig. 3-2).

 Since a stranded raft is low in the water, it is important to have a flare capable of reaching high altitudes. A flare would enable a ship out of your line of sight to be alerted, particularly in instances where because of the curvature of the earth, the use of other types of signaling devices would be ineffective. Flares that can attain great heights (such as the parachute, rocket and meteor flare) provide a longer and more conspicuous signal to the distant viewer.

Consider the following example:

At a distance of 21 miles, a meteor flare that is 250 feet above sea level will appear to the viewer as a brief signal on the surface of the ocean, because of the earth's curvature. This same flare, at a distance of only ten miles, will appear to be about 125 feet above the surface (consequently producing a longer burn period of visibility for sighting and confirmation). In the case of a parachute flare at 1000 feet altitude, a viewer from a distance of 41 miles will see only a brief signal of light on the surface or horizon of the ocean.

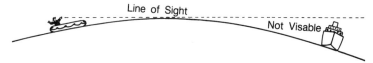

Fig. 3-2 *Due to the curvature of the earth, the survivor should be aware that sighting distances are limited.*

Whereas from half that distance, 20 miles, the flare will appear to be at about 500 feet altitude and will be visible for a considerably longer time (Fig. 3-3).

Signals that can be seen at high altitudes are generally better to use when distance is a factor.

Locate Signals

Locate signals include any device that will provide and/or maintain a signal long enough for an approaching craft to get a fix on you. Your goal is to create a signal that a ship or aircraft can "home in" on.

Many distress devices can accomplish both alert and locate functions. A mirror, for example, can be used to alert an aircraft, as well as to furnish a constant signal, (weather permitting) for the aircraft to home in on. It is a good idea to have adequate supplies of both types of signals to increase your chances of rescue.

VISUAL SIGNALING DEVICES

The following signaling devices may vary from one manufacturer to another. Each manufacturer will provide its own operating instructions, which should be adhered to.

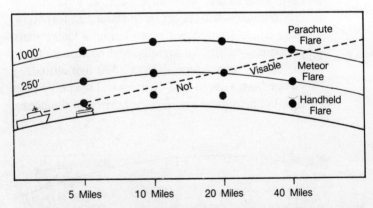

Fig. 3-3 The above diagram illustrates the height at which various types of signal flares will be visible.

Pyrotechnics

Orange Smoke Flares. These flares are designed for daytime use and provide one of the best signals for locating. They are hand-held, and have a burn time of about 50 to 90 seconds, depending upon the model. Some are equipped with wooden handles, are waterproof, and have flotation capabilities.

Red or Bright-White Flares. These are primarily for nighttime use. At night a smoke flare would be virtually invisible. These handheld devices have a candlepower of about 500 and an approximate burn time of 2 minutes.

Highway Flares. These produce a red light and have a lengthy burn time. They are much less expensive than the regular marine flares, but they produce a considerably smaller amount of light (approximately 70 candlepower). These flares are not Coast Guard approved, and one disadvantage is that they produce a hot sulfur ash that can be a hazard.

Aerial Flares

Handheld Rocket Flares. These are generally of two types: low altitude with a short burn span, and high altitude with a long burn span.

Pen Gun Flares. A 45-caliber cartridge is screwed into the end of the pen gun and fired by a spring-loaded pin. The flare generates a candle power of 4000, and attains altitudes of 450 to 500 feet.

Pistol Launched Flares. These are generally available in 12 gauge, 25mm, and 37mm. They produce a candlepower of 10,000. They are also referred to as meteor flares, and are capable of alerting distant ships from as far away as 20 miles and aircraft at around 10 miles, depending on atmospheric conditions. A parachute equipped rocket flare that is capable of reaching altitudes of 1,000 feet can have a burn time of 60 seconds or longer (Fig. 3-4).

Note: Rocket flares capable of reaching even greater

Fig. 3-4 An alert/locate device: Flare Gun. (Photo courtesy OLIN.)

heights with longer burn times are available, but are more costly.

Colored Dye Markers

Colored dye markers are used primarily as a locating device. The powdered dye is dispursed on the ocean surface around the raft. The marker is usually bright orange and can be detected from as far away as 10 miles by aircraft on a clear day. Because it remains on the surface of the ocean for a period of time, it is more noticable from the air than from other craft at sea level, and will last longest in smooth seas.

Heliograph (Mirrors)

The reflection of a mirror or shiny object is very noticable on the ocean, and the fact that it is reusable increases its value as a signaling device. The mirror should have a sighting hole in the middle and reflection capabilities on both sides, for maximum efficiency and to allow for proper aim on the target.

Flags or Panels

Flags or panels that are brightly colored are used for both alert and locate purposes. They emphasize a contrast to the ocean's background (a bright orange life raft canopy would accomplish this even more effectively.) The distress panel, although it takes up more space than the flag, is less influenced by the wind (or lack of it), and is also reflective under a search light.

Strobe Light

A strobe light is a high intensity flashing light. It can be used for both alert and locating purposes. The blue/white light flashes about once every second. These waterproof units are small in weight and size, and can be easily attached to gear or person. Most are equipped with off/on switches (gravity activated or water activated).

Whistle

A whistle is an extremely effective locator signal for man-overboard situations. If you've fallen overboard, your voice may be virtually useless as a signaling device, especially in conditions of rough weather or fog. A whistle attached to your PFD (and Man-Over-Board Pole) will dramatically increase your chances of being heard and located. It is best to use a plastic whistle that won't corrode.

RADIO AND TELEGRAPH DEVICES

Since the advent of electricity, man has endeavored to improve his communications systems on national and international levels. The high priority given to improving national military defense has resulted in vast technological advances in this field. The by-product of this development is a much broader spectrum and choice of communication gear for the modern sailor that has effectively lengthened his contact to shore.

Despite these advances, the isolated survivor still faces immense odds while adrift on the open ocean. Possession of a radio does not ensure contact, just as contact does not guarantee rescue. Nevertheless, the off-shore sailor should take advantage of the sophisticated communication systems available today to maximize his chance of rescue.

EPIRB

The EPIRB (Emergency Position Indicating Radio Beacon) is a modified version of the earlier aviation ELT (Emergency Locating Transmitter). It is usually equipped with both a manual and a salt water activating system. This self-contained battery-operated unit transmits an inaudible, electric oscillating or "swept" tone (Figs. 3-5 through 3-7).

The EPIRB transmits on the Civil VHF distress frequency of 121.5 MHz (also the aviation distress frequency) and on the military UHF distress frequency of 243.0 MHz. The effective range can vary with atmospheric conditions and battery charge. Aircraft can pick up the signal from 200 to 300 miles away, but the range at sea level is considerably less (Fig. 3-8).

The beacon is capable of transmitting a continuous

Fig. 3-5 E.P.I.R.B. — Emergency Position Radio Indicating Beacon. (Photo courtesy The Guest Corporation).

Fig. 3-6 Mini Class B EPIRB (Photo courtesy ACR Electronics, Inc.)

distress signal 24 hours a day for the life of the batteries. The important benefit of an EPIRB is that the survivor need not be awake or be able to see the rescue vessel in order to alert it. The models available are basically similar in function. Some contain voice capabilities for transmitting and receiving, water-activated switches, flotation capabilities, as well as other optional features that may vary according to price.

Search and Rescue Satellites

The latest in search and rescue technology is a new type of satellite called SARSATS (Search and Rescue Satellite). These space crafts are equipped with special re-

Fig. 3-7 Class A EPIRB for Attachment to lifecraft. (Courtesy ACR Electronic, Inc.)

ceivers that are tuned to standard international distress frequencies. Once orbiting, these satellites are capable of receiving distress transmissions from inexpensive emergency beacons almost any where on earth.

The first use of one such satellite was the Russian Cosmos 1,387. While in orbit the Soviet SARSAT picked up a distress signal from a downed aircraft in the wilderness of British Columbia. The transmission from the aircraft's automatic emergency beacon was relayed from the satellite to an antenna outside Ottawa where a computer quickly obtained a navigational fix on the crash site enabling rescue within hours.

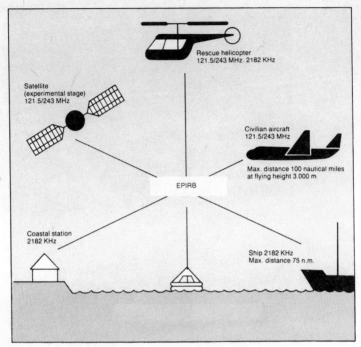

Fig. 3-8 Various monitoring frequencies for search & rescue.

Radio Telephones (Transceivers)

Generally used in coastal waters, the VHF radio (Very High Frequency) comprises the majority of radio equipment on the average boat. VHF transmissions are "line of sight" and consequently limited by the curvature of the earth. The radio is equipped with numerous crystals or channels, depending upon the model, but all of them are equipped with channel 16, the guarded distress frequency of 156.8 MHz that is monitored by the coast guard around the clock. This frequency is also monitored by other vessels.

All radio telephones require an FCC (Federal Communications Commission) station license and all transmitting operators are required to have an FCC operators permit.

The citizens band (CB or class D radio) is available in various sizes and vary according to price. These are low powered transmit/receivers that are limited in distance.

Because of its relatively low frequency, and the wide abuse by the public in certain areas, the CB is not recognized as a legitimate emergency device by the Coast Guard. Nevertheless, because of the popularity and wide use of the CB, channel 9 is frequently monitored by the Coast Guard as an emergency channel.

Radio Distress Frequencies

The following is a list of U.S. and international distress frequencies that are guarded and monitored:

- Radiotelegraph
    Distress frequency: 500 KHz
- Radiotelephones
    VHF distress frequency: 121.5 MHz (The beacon distress frequency for aviation as well as shipping).
    UHF Military distress frequency: 243.0 MHz.
    Channel 16, VHF radio: (standard coastal type) distress frequency is 156.8 MHz.

USING DISTRESS SIGNALS

The signal devices just listed normally provide operating instructions printed directly on the device itself. These instructions should be understood before you need to use the signal in an emergency. This understanding will help save precious moments during the emergency and will enable you to know how to use the signals even if the instructions become illegible.

SIGNALING DEVICE LIMITATIONS

The necessity of having a balanced supply of both alert-type and location-type signal equipment cannot be over-emphasized. The limitations inherent in each of the following signaling devices may not only compromise their effectiveness but can also render them useless in some situations.

Daytime Smoke Flare. These flares are adversely affected by poor visibility. They are also difficult for the rescue craft to see if it must look directly into the sun to see the flare.

Flag. Flags are influenced by wind direction and lack of wind. If the rescue boat is located directly upwind or downwind, flags will be more difficult to spot.

Lights. Lights (strobe, flash, etc.) are effective only at night.

Whistle or Horn. The most obvious limitation of a whistle or horn is distance. Your position in relation to the wind direction and the rescue vessel will also influence their effectiveness.

Mirror. Mirrors are restricted to daytime use only, with the requirement that there be a workable angle between the sun and your mirror, and the sun and the rescue craft.

Radio Beacon. A necessary requirement for a radio beacon is that the potential rescue craft be equipped with a receiver with direction finding capabilities.

Dye. Dye is adversely affected by limited visibility at sea level. It also dissipates quickly in rough seas.

Parachute, Meteor, and Rocket Flares. These types of flares are difficult to see against bright sunlight.

By illustrating the multiple uses of signaling devices, and more importantly their individual limitations, the necessity of having a full complement of signaling devices on board should be apparent to the conscientious yachtsman.

SIGNAL PROVISIONS

There is a general consensus as to what type of signaling devices should be included in basic provisions, but opinions vary as to quantities. The decision as to how much of each item to include is influenced by available space, your budget, and priority evaluations.

Weigh your decisions objectively and reach a balance that will fit your particular situation without compromising your safety. The loss or malfunction of vital equipment in stressful situations is well documented.

MAINTENANCE AND STORAGE

Most distress signals have a substantial shelf life and require little maintenance. Batteries should be changed at least every 3 months, and light bulbs should also be checked and replaced if necessary. Salt water activated batteries have a longer shelf life than other types of batteries, if they are properly protected from moisture. Distress signals should be replaced according to the expiration date printed on them.

Storage should be given high priority in terms of location and accessibility. Distress signals should be stored in a location that allows for protection against the elements and tampering, but that also allows for instant availability in an emergency.

If your supply of distress signals cannot be kept in the life raft itself, (as in the case of the inflatable life raft packed in its container), then they should be securely packed and stored in an accessible location. The entire crew should be informed as to their whereabouts, and should realize the importance of successfully transfering them to the life raft in an emergency.

Distress signals should be packed in a floatable container. This will guard against loss should nervous hands slip while transferring supplies to the dinghy or raft. If you have to toss it overboard, its flotation capabilities will allow you to retrieve it later.

MAYDAY PROCEDURES

Radiotelegraph, as well as most other signaling methods use the Morse code to signal distress. This is, three short signals, three long, then three short again . . . pause, and repeat. This is written as dot dot dot, dash dash dash, dot dot dot:

. . . - - - . . .

The spoken mayday for radiotelephone is simply: "Mayday, mayday, mayday" spoken three times preceding any transmission or message. Then continue with the message. If possible, begin with "this is an emergency" and then give the following information:

1. Your vessel's name and radio call letters.
2. The nature of your distress call (sinking, fire, abandoning ship, injury, etc.)
3. Your location: latitude/longitude and any additional information such as: last port of call, length of time out of last port, bearings to nearby beacons or land features, and any other information that would help locate and identify you.
4. Description of your vessel: sail/power, length, color of hull/trim, or any helpful or distinguishing markings.
5. Repeat the above information and then proceed to give the following information:
   • Number of persons aboard.
   • Type of assistance required.
   • Prospective course, wind directions, weather conditions, and current directions.
   • Survival equipment and signaling devices available to you.

SIGNALING SKILLS

It is advisable to wait until you see or hear a vessel or aircraft before using a signal so you do not waste your supply of signals.

Once the potential rescue vessel is sighted and alerted, consider the distance that the vessel must travel to reach you. Make sure you ration the use of your locate signals in accordance with the distance the rescue boat must travel to reach you.

Refer to the manufacturer's operating instructions before activating any distress signal.

Emergency Radio

When using your emergency radio, monitor and transmit on the hour and half hour.

Use your battery power conservatively when using battery operated radios. Reserve some energy to provide search and rescue craft with a RDF (Radio Direction Finder) signal that they can home in on.

Search and rescue authorities agree that EPIRBS should be left on continuously, once activated.

Pyrotechnics

Handheld Flares. Be sure to use handheld flares properly and be aware of their potential as a fire hazard. Don't wave handheld flares (Fig. 3-9). Use flares appropriately: smoke flares are for daytime use, red or bright burning light flares are for nighttime use.

Projectile Flares. When signaling with alert-type devices, it may be more effective to fire them in tandem.

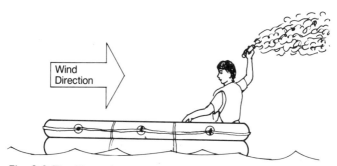

Fig. 3-9 The illustration indicates the correct way to hold flares for effective and safe signaling.

This specifically applies to meteor aerial flares (fire the first flare, then when it dissipates or extinguishes, fire the second one immediately). This type of sequence firing will provide a better signal for confirmation of the sighting and/or the direction.

Parachute-type flares need not be fired in tandem, as their burn times are considerably longer and most likely sufficient for an alert and confirmation.

Heliograph

Anything that is shiny or reflective on both sides can be used as a signaling mirror. To aim effectively, put a hole or "crosshole" of about ¼ inch in the center of the mirror, tin can, chrome piece, or whatever you are using.

- To use a heliograph, you must have a workable angle between the sun, your mirror, and the rescue craft.
- From the air, the flash from a mirror can be seen from 10 to 40 miles on a clear day.
- Even if you can only hear a plane in the distance, begin signaling with the mirror. An airplane will be able to see the flash of light before you can see the plane.
- Once the pilot has acknowledged your signal and has located you, be careful not to blind him by continuing to flash the mirror.

Practice with the mirror to improve aim rather than to wait until a "sighting" to use it the first time. Aiming can be difficult in rough water or "down-sun" angles (Fig. 3-10).

To correctly aim the mirror, hold it 3 to 4 inches from your face and sight the ship or plane through the hole in the mirror. The ray of sunlight coming through the hole onto your face can be seen in the reflective back side of the mirror. Move the mirror slowly until the spot of light from your cheek disappears into the hole, while at the same

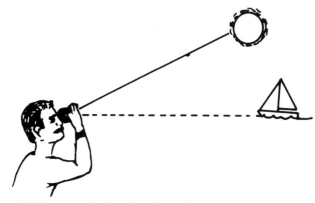

Fig. 3-10 Proper technique for effectively using a signal mirror.

time keeping the rescue craft visible through the hole. The sun will then be properly reflected on the target.

USE YOUR SIGNALS WISELY

When a vessel is sighted on the horizon, pause for a moment and try to assess its course. Rather than using up flares in a panicked fashion at the mere sight of the ship, try to decipher its course and then wait until it appears to be at its closest point. This is the point at which it will be most effective to signal the vessel.

Any distress device that is reusable such as a heliograph or a radio should be used first. This will prevent the possible waste of one-time use signals. Effective signaling will depend, of course, on the situation and your perception of it, but always try to use your signaling stores wisely and efficiently.

4

Weather

ASSESSING APPROACHING WEATHER AND changes in weather is difficult, even with sophisticated equipment. In the survival situation, the only course of action is to observe the weather and try to prepare for it, both mentally and physically.

Approaching weather cannot be altered, and unless your survival craft has sailing capabilities, it will be virtually impossible to avoid any oncoming weather. No matter what actions you take the weather will run its course. Correctly reading the approach of a storm, for instance, is of obvious value. It is more advantageous to the survivor afloat to be able to determine if clouds will yield rain.

Without having a radio with receiving capabilities, the only immediate criteria available to determine weather information is the following:

- Cloud patterns and formations
- Wind direction and intensity
- Swell size and direction
- Temperature changes

Studying cloud patterns and development is probably the best and easiest method available to the novice. Clouds are a visible sign of moisture in the air and their formation provides important clues to weather conditions.

Large masses of air in the earth's midlatitudes generally move in a west to east direction. Therefore, look to the west for signs of approaching weather and clouds that herald change. During the winter these air masses can attain speeds of 30 miles per hour covering about 700 miles a day. During summertime speeds can reach about 20 miles per hour, reaching 500 miles per day.

The following photos represent an example of the basic cloud genera and the typical conditions that result from them. Exceptions will always prevail but evidence shows that a high degree of consistency is present.

CLOUDS

High Clouds

Predominantly composed of ice crystals
Cirrus (curl) (Fig. 4-1):

Fig. 4-1 Cirrus Cloud Formations. (Photo courtesy NOAA)

- Generally white in color
- Delicate in appearance
- Composed of ice crystals
- Appear as:
  1. Dense patches with frayed borders
  2. Rounded tufts or hooks
  3. Long thin lines reaching across the sky
  4. Plume-like and feathery at times
- Generally related to fair weather, but could be the forerunner of rain if they are followed by lower and thicker clouds.

Cirrocumulus (Mackerel sky) (Fig. 4-2):

- Comprised of scales or white flakes, or globular masses
- Honeycomb appearance
- Resemble ripples in sand
- Commonly known as "mackerel sky" due to patterns resembling the scales on the back of a mackerel

Fig. 4-2 Cirrocumulus Cloud Formations. (Photo courtesy NOAA)

- Layers show very slight vertical development
- Generally associated with fair weather, but if they thicken and lower wind and rain may follow

Cirrostratus: (Fig. 4-3):

- Contains an abundance of ice crystals
- Light refraction produces luminous tangent arc or "halo" effect in the sky
- Thin whitish transparent veil or web completely covering the sky
- Commonly known "mares' tails" result from cirrus thickening and becoming cirrostratus.
- If thickening continues the ice crystals will melt to form water droplets, known as altostratus, and you may expect rain within 24 hours

Middle Clouds

Altocumulus (Fig. 4-4):

- Composed of water droplets with ice crystals forming only at very low temperatures

Fig. 4-3 Cirrostratus Cloud Formation. (Photo courtesy NOAA)

Fig. 4-4 Altocumulus Cloud Formation. (Photo courtesy NOAA)

- Usually seen as a sheet of regularly arranged cloudlets
- Known as "sheep backs" or "castles in the air"
- White and gray and appear rounded
- Often mistaken for stratocumulus
- Masses tend to merge together
- Occasionally appear shortly before a thunderstorm
- Usually indicate a change to unstable and thundery skies

Altostratus (Fig. 4-5):

- Composed of water droplets, raindrops, snowflakes, and ice crystals
- Bluish or grayish cloud sheet, veil or layer in fibrous or uniform appearance
- The sun or moon appears as though shining through "ground glass"
- Halos are not present
- Continuous rain or snow may be expected within a few hours if these clouds thicken and lower, or if rain clouds

Fig. 4-5 Altostratus Cloud Formation. (Photo courtesy NOAA)

(nimbostratus) form below them appearing as a sort of "ragged scud"

Low Clouds

Stratocumulus (Fig. 4-6):

- Composed of water drops except in extreme cold weather
- Gray and whitish cloud layers with dark patches
- Soft in appearance
- Their motion is similar to ocean waves
- Vary greatly in altitude

Fig. 4-6 Stratocumulus Cloud Formation. (Photo courtesy NOAA)

- Usually clear skies will follow during the night

Stratus (Fig. 4-7):

- Gray cloud layer with uniform base
- Resembles fog
- Produces drizzle or mist
- Stratus family clouds have a base that is below 1000 feet and becomes "fog" when on the ground

Nimbostratus (Fig. 4-8):

- Dark, gray cloud layer, thick enough to blot out the sun
- Continuous precipitation
- No electric or thunderous activity
- Shapeless cloud layer
- Typical rain cloud

Fig. 4-7 Stratus Cloud Formation. (Photo courtesy NOAA)

Vertical Clouds

Cumulus (Fig. 4-9):

- Generally dense and detached
- Developing as rising mounds or towers

Fig. 4-8 Nimbostratus Cloud Formation. (Photo courtesy NOAA)

Fig. 4-9 Cumulus Cloud Formation. (Photo courtesy NOAA)

- Brilliant white on top with a horizontal and somewhat dark base
- Dome shaped upper surface
- Commonly known as "woolpack" clouds
- Usually accompany fair weather

Fig. 4-10 Cumulonimbus Cloud Formations. (Photo courtesy NOAA)

Cumulonimbus (Fig. 4-10):

- Massive cloud pattern with anvil shape at top
- Reaches great heights
- Upper portion is formed of ice crystals
- Base is dark, horizontal, and becomes lower and ragged as showers occur
- Commonly known as thundercloud or thunderhead

RAIN CLOUDS

Your ability to recognize rain clouds is valuable because it is extremely important to take advantage of any conditions that will provide you with water. Water stores should be updated and topped off with fresh water whenever possible. If you are convinced that an approaching cloud will rain on you, it may be wise to issue extra water rations to the crew and drink some of the water in your stores in order to provide greater space for any fresh water you catch.

Proper recognition of a rain cloud will also allow you extra time to prepare for a new rainfall, and thus avoid having to waste time rigging a catchment during the rainfall.

LIGHTNING

- When lightning is sighted in the distance there is a delay before hearing the thunder. The approximate distance of the lightning and storm in relation to where you are can be calculated by the following simple formula:

> From the moment you see the lightning, count the seconds until you hear the thunder. To ascertain the distance in statute miles, divide the number of seconds by 5; it takes roughly that long for sound to travel over one mile. For the same distance in nautical miles divide the number by 5.5.

FOG

Fog is basically a cloud with its base on or near the surface of the ocean. Its occurance is relatively rare at the equator or in the trade wind belt (with the exception of the coasts of California, Chili, Northwest and Southwest Africa).

Fog can have definite effects on your judgement in terms of distance and sound. If you are approaching a shore and are unable to see it because of a heavy fog layer, listen sharply for the break of waves on the shore. Remember that the sound you hear may be distorted from the layer of fog.

GENERAL CIRCULATION OF EARTH'S ATMOSPHERE

Briefly simplified, the general circulation of the earth's atmosphere results from the sun's effect on the earth's surface, and the atmospheric temperatures. A low pressure belt occurs near the equatorial latitudes. This belt, called the doldrums, is approximately midway between two high pressure belts. The surface airs of the earth tend to move from an area of high pressure to that of an area of low pressure (Fig. 4-11).

Doldrums

Doldrums is the belt of low pressure near the equator. The area is located between the north and south trade winds. This area experiences frequent showers and thundershowers and is often overcast. There may be prolonged periods of time without wind. Light winds that do blow are often inconsistent and vary in direction. Hot and sultry days are a common occurance. Except for slight changes, the atmospheric pressure along the equatorial trough is almost uniform.

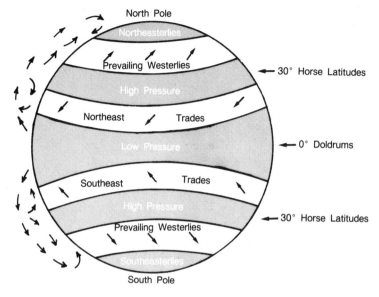

Fig. 4-11 General circulation of the earth's atmosphere.

Trade Wind Belt

The trade winds are considered the most constant of winds. They are not necessarily continuous but are markedly more consistent with regard to season. In all areas they are "fresher" during the winter months than during the summer.

Trades blow from belts of high pressure to the equatorial belts of lower pressure. Trade winds in the northern hemisphere will come from the northeast, called the northeast trades. Trade winds in the southern hemisphere will come from the southeast, and are called the southeast trades.

Horse Latitudes

On the poleward side of each trade wind belt, and corresponding roughly with the zone of high pressure in each hemisphere, is an area with weak pressure gradients and variable winds. This region is called the horse latitudes. Unlike the weather in the doldrums, the weather in the horse latitudes is fresh and usually clear.

Westerlies

In the northern summer, the westerly wind belts are 35 degrees to about 65 degrees north, in the southern hemisphere summer 36 degrees to 65 degrees south. They are stronger in their perspective winters and stronger in the southern band. Their actual wind direction is variable from north-west to south-west. The variations in wind is due to a series of depressions passing through the area. Because there is less land interference in the southern hemisphere, the southern westerlies are stronger and are often referred to as the roaring forties.

Polar Winds

Temperatures near the geographic poles are low, and because of this, pressure tends to remain higher at the poles than in the surrounding regions. The polar winds blow outward from the poles and are deflected west by the earth's rotation. They become known as the northeasterlies in the Arctic and the southeasterlies in the Antarctic.

General Rule: Buys Ballot's Law

If an observer in the northern hemisphere faces the wind, the center of low pressure is toward his right, and somewhat behind him; the center of high pressure is toward his left and somewhat in front of him.

If an observer in the southern hemisphere faces the wind, the center of low pressure is toward his left and somewhat behind him; and the center of high pressure is toward his right and somewhat in front of him.

Fronts

On weather maps, the boundary zones of different air masses are drawn in as lines, which are called weather fronts, or simply fronts. A front may be regarded as a line dividing two different air masses. The boundaries between air masses are really zones of transition, ranging from 5 to 60 miles in width. Weather fronts have been classified into a simple system for study:

- Cold Front—a front along which colder air replaces warmer air
- Warm Front—a front along which warmer air replaces colder air
- Occluded Front—a front resulting when a cold front over takes a warm front and the warm air is forced aloft
- Stationary Front—a front along which one air mass does not replace another air mass

Squall Lines

Squall lines, sometimes called instability lines, are extremely dangerous phenomena for small boats, and should be avoided, if at all possible. Squall lines are narrow zones of instability that sometimes occur 50 to 300 miles ahead of a fast-moving cold front. The development of squall lines takes place when winds above a cold frontal surface are moving in the same direction as the cold front, but at greater speed, and prevent the warm air ahead of the cold front from rising. Violent weather, extreme gustiness, and downpours often occur just behind the squall line.

Beaufort Wind Scale

The Beaufort wind scale has been in general use for more than a hundred years. Most yachtsmen stick to the Beaufort scale for quoting wind strength because it was designed for sailing ships (Table 4-1).

Table 4-1.

Beaufort Number	Speed Knots	Land m.p.h.	Description	Height of Waves
0	0	0	Calm	—
1	2	2.3	Light air. Ruffles with the appearance of scales.	—
2	5	5.8	Light breeze. Small wavelets, still short, but more pronounced. Crests do not break.	½
3	9	10.3	Gentle breeze. Large wavelets' crests begin to break. Perhaps scattered white horses.	2
4	13	15	Moderate breeze. Small waves becoming longer. Frequent white horses.	4
5	18	20.7	Fresh Breeze. Moderate wave take a pronounces long form. Many white horses.	6
6	24	27.6	Strong breeze. Larger wave form; foam crests more extensive.	9
7	30	34.5	Moderate gale. Seas heap up; white foam from beaking waves begins to be blown with wind.	13
8	37	42.6	Fresh gale. Moderate high waves; edges of crests break into spindrift. Foam blown into well maked streaks. Spray reduces visibility.	18
9	44	50.6	Strong gale. High waves. Dense streaks of foam. Spray affects visibility.	23
10	51	58.7	Whole gale. Very high waves with long overhanging crests. Dense white foam. Whole surface of sea streaks takes white appearance.	30
11	60	69	Storm. Exceptionally high waves. Sea completely covered with long white patches of foam. (Small ships lost to view behind waves.) Everywhere, the edges of wave crests are blown into froth. Visibility poor.	40 or more
12	—	—	Hurricane. Air filled with foam and spray. Sea completely white with spray. Visibility seriously affected.	40 or more

5

Exposure: Hypothermia and Dehydration

ABOUT HYPOTHERMIA

Hypothermia is one of the greatest immediate threats to the castaway in a survival situation. Hypothermia is a physiological condition caused by exposure that results in the lowering of the body's core temperature. Acute or advanced hypothermia occurs when the body is losing more heat than it can generate. Extreme prolonged loss of body heat will result in acute hypothermia and eventually death.

Hypothermia and the Body

The body's heating system is based upon what is known as the *basal metabolic rate*. This is a complex heat production system that maintains a balanced body temperature. The body's heat production system responds to hypothermia by increasing the metabolic rate to compensate or counteract the large heat loss. The body's initial defense, intense shivering, serves to generate and increase the amount of heat in the body, but because it requires energy to shiver, it will eventually cause fatigue.

As exposure to cold continues, the body's natural priority is to maintain a normal level of heat within the core of the body. The body's defense systems automatically work to protect the temperature level of the inner core by sacrificing the extremities: hands, feet, legs, and arms. Numbness occurs in these areas as blood vessels close to the skin contract.

This contraction of blood vessels causes less blood to flow through those areas that are coldest. In this way, the amount of "cold" blood that will return to the inner core and threaten the vital organs is reduced. The head is a vital organ, and consequently there is no blood vessel constriction occurring to reduce the amount of blood going to the head. This is why the greatest amount of body heat loss during exposure is from the head.

Case studies have shown that persons who appear to be dead from hypothermia or drowning in cold water can sometimes be resuscitated successfully even after a considerable period without breathing and blood circulation sometimes for as long as 10 to 40 minutes. The primary reason for this is that body tissues require less oxygen when cold than when warm. Therefore, don't give up! Maintain artificial ventilation and circulation on a hypothermic victim as long as possible.

Statistics

Figure 5-1 shows average predicted survival times of an adult in water of different temperatures.

The figures are based on data compiled at the University of Victoria. The scientists studied experimental cooling of average men and women who were holding still in ocean water and wearing a standard lifejacket and light clothing. The graph shows, for example, that predicted survival time is about 2½ to 3 hours in water of 50°F Fahrenheit (10°C).

Predicted survival time is increased by extra body fat and decreased by small body size. Although women usually

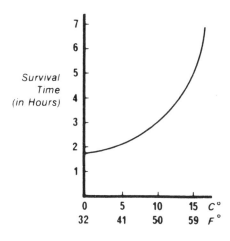

Fig. 5-1 Survival time in cold water. (Courtesy Mustang.)

possess slightly more fat than men, they often cool faster because of their generally smaller body size. Children cool much faster than adults because of smaller body mass and relatively little fat.

The warmest ocean waters near the equator reach temperatures of about 82 degrees Fahrenheit. Since a healthy body temperature stays around 98 degrees, prolonged immersion or exposure to water that is cooler than 98 degrees can result in hypothermia. This of course will depend upon the length of exposure, but it should be understood that the hypothermic process will begin lowering your body temperature immediately.

Table 5-1, compiled by NOAA (National Oceanic and Atmospheric Administration), indicates how the approximate survival time of human beings in the sea is directly related to sea surface temperatures.

HYPOTHERMIA: SYMPTOMS, TREATMENT, PREVENTION

The most effective safeguard against hypothermia is to understand what it is and how to prevent it. Although the possibility of hypothermia is obviously greater in cold cli-

Table 5-1. Approximate Survival Time in the Sea Related to the Sea Temperature

Water Temperature		Exhaustion/ Unconsciousness	Expected Time of Survival
Centigrade	Fahrenheit		
0.3	32.5	15 minutes	15–45 hours
0.3–4.4	32.5–40	15–30 minutes	30–90 hours
4.4–10	40–50	30–60 minutes	1–3 hours
10–15.6	50–60	1–2 hours	1–6 hours
15.6–21.1	60–70	27 hours	2–40 hours
21.1–26.7	70–80	Indefinitely	Indefinitely

mates, hypothermia can be a danger in any climate, no matter how amiable the air and water temperatures seem to be. Hypothermia can be a significant threat to survival, even in the tropics.

CAUSES

Heat loss will occur any time the body is in contact or exposed to lower temperatures. Prolonged contact of your body to the floor of a life raft while adrift in cold water, for example, can chill you by transferring your body heat outward through the floor of the raft. This is why a double floor or insulating material in a life raft is particularly important in colder climates.

Exposure to the wind will also accelerate hypothermia, as will the wearing of wet clothing, especially in cold climates. During immersion in cold water, clothing can help by serving to "trap" and keep the water warmed by your body, next to the skin. But once you are out of the water, do not wear wet clothing. Obviously, wet clothing is preferable to no clothing, but you should at least make an attempt to remove the clothes wring them out, and then put them on again.

Wet clothes are no longer an efficient insulator, and instead of trapping warm air next to the skin, they conduct body heat outwardly and away from the skin. Strenuous activity in cold climates can also result in sweat saturated clothing, which must be considered a threat and dealt with accordingly.

Symptoms

Shivering. Shivering is uncontrollable. Intense shivering follows in an attempt to increase the body's heat production and counteract the large heat loss.

Loss of Awareness. Difficulty of speech, confusion of thought, and amnesia are all signs of loss of awareness.

Rigidity. Muscular rigidity replaces shivering. The

person is semiconscious in appearance and the skin turns bluish and puffy.

Pulse Slows. The pulse in extremities is almost non-existent. The pulse should be taken from the carotid (neck) artery.

Unconsciousness. Erratic heartbeat, lack of reflexes, and dilation of pupils are signs of unconsciousness. Unconsciousness can occur when the body's "core" temperature falls from the normal 99°F (37°C) to approximately 86°F (32°C). (Fig 5-2).

Relaxation. The victim experiences overall muscular relaxation and is similar in appearance to death.

Respiratory Control Failure.

Cardiac Failure. Heart failure is the usual cause of death when inner core temperature cools to intolerable levels.

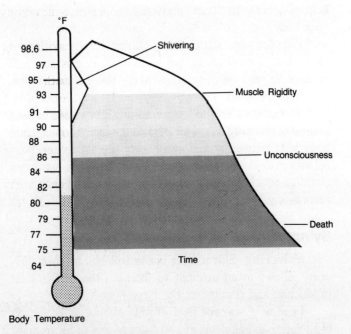

°F

98.6
97
95
93
91
90
88
86
84
82
80
79
77
75
64

Shivering

Muscle Rigidity

Unconsciousness

Death

Time

Body Temperature

Fig. 5-2 The graph indicates the relative length of survival for decreasing body temperatures.

Treatment

In the advanced stage of hypothermia, the body has lost its ability to rewarm itself. The natural treatment is to introduce or replace warmth back into the body. Caution must be used, however, as many standard techniques of introducing warmth are dangerous and may only aggravate the condition.

In the case of an unconscious survivor, for example, massage, exercise, or any stimulation of blood circulation will only serve to worsen the condition. Such actions hasten the flow of cold blood from the numb extremities to the heart, causing a further drop in body temperature.

The most effective treatment is to introduce warmth into the core of the body by warm or hot liquids, or warmed oxygen. This heating of the body from the inside-out is the only safe way to counteract advanced hypothermia.

Because hot liquids or oxygen are rarely available in the survival raft, the following is a list of tips and techniques that may be effective in controlling hypothermia:

Terminate Exposure. If possible, remove the victim from the water. Dry off or wring out wet clothes immediately. Stay out of the wind. Close the canopy openings to retain body generated warmth. Huddle together or, if alone, curl up into a fetal position.

Body Contact (warmth). Body-to-body contact may be the only source of warmth available. Extreme caution must be exercised to ensure that the other survivors don't become chilled and hypothermic in the process.

Hot Liquids. Hot liquids is a most effective treatment, but never give liquids to an unconscious person. If possible, administer a hot bath.

Forced Exercise. If the survivor is still conscious try to get him to move around a bit.

Allow No Alcohol. Consuming alcohol will cause the blood vessels to dilate. This will allow more blood to flow into the cold extremities, causing a quicker return of cold blood to the inner core of the body.

Rations. Allow the victim to eat extra rations, if available, specifically carbohydrates.

Allow No Smoking. The nicotine in cigarettes will cause the blood vessels to constrict, which will impede and reduce the flow of warmed blood to the colder areas, such as the hands and feet.

Prevention

The treatment and prevention of hypothermia are very similar. Each situation dictates the degree to which you can be successful in counteracting hypothermia. The object is to maintain your body heat.

The balance of body heat is maintained by either the regulation of heat loss, or by the body's production of heat. Heat production can be increased by food digestion or exercise, but both are limited measures. The most effective preventive measure is to reduce and regulate the amount of heat loss. Here are some tips to keep in mind:

- Understand the conditions that encourage hypothermia.
- Protect yourself to the best of your ability against cold, wind, and wetness.
- Pay particular attention to protecting your extremities: head, nose, ears, feet, and hands. Great amounts of body heat can be lost through these areas.
- Try to retain body heat by huddling, curling up, closing the canopy, etc.
- Drink hot liquids, whenever possible, to heat the body from the inside out.
- Exercise muscles. Rub your hands, stretch your feet, move your body around, and keep your blood circulating.
- Clothing, if dry, will insulate the body by creating a dead

air space between your skin and the inner garment. A tightly fitting garment will reduce the size of the air pocket or dead air zone, which will consequently reduce the amount of warmth retained. Loose fitting clothing is better, but not so loose that it exposes your body to wind drafts.

- In cold climates, control your sweating when engaged in vigorous activity. Sweat saturated garments conduct heat away from your body and can further the hypothermic process.

IMMERSION IN COLD WATER

If you are wearing a flotation device, less body heat will be lost by remaining still in the water rather than swimming or treading water. Curling up into a fetal position will increase your survival time.

Because about 50 percent of your body heat is lost from the head area, try to keep your head as far out of the water as possible and turn your back to the waves and wind. Covering your head with a hood will help conserve body heat.

If there are several people in the water, huddling close together can help preserve body heat (Fig. 5-3).

PARADOXICAL COOLING

Guard against paradoxical cooling. This refers to the dangerous condition resulting when a survivor has been warmed by external methods. His skin's surface may feel warm to the touch and he will tell you that he feels better, but in fact, his inner core temperature is still dropping dangerously.

- It can often take hours to restore all of the lost body heat. Fatalities of this kind are particularly tragic, and result from neglect and a general misunderstanding of the hypothermic process. Hot liquids or warmed oxygen are the most effective treatment against paradoxical cooling.

Fig. 5-3 Survivors should huddle close together to maintain body heat.

DEHYDRATION

Dehydration, which is the loss of body fluids, is another serious threat to the castaway who may find himself faced with either a limited or nonexistent water supply.

Dehydration can occur in either cold or hot environments, but exposure to tropical heat can seriously accelerate the process because of the effect that high temperature has on the body's metabolic process. The dehydration process is triggered as fluid is lost in the body through excessive sweating when the body tries to cool itself down.

If the dehydration process continues without fluid intake, it will result in acute dehydration and eventually death. Excessive sweating can also create a dangerously low salt level in the body. This sweating alters the consistency of the blood causing cramps in the limbs and abdomen.

Because dehydration is such a grave threat to the castaway, the mariner must have an ample supply of water and water collecting devices in his survival provisions. This is especially crucial in geographical areas where rainfall is scarce or seasonal.

Symptoms

- Lassitude and apathy
- Loss of appetite
- Drowsiness and sluggishness, headache
- Acute thirst, very dry mouth, cracked lips
- Slowness of speech
- Weakness of legs

Treatment

The treatment for dehydration is simply to increase the intake of water until the process is reversed. Anyone suffering from dehydration should increase his water ration, if supplies permit.

Because water is often the most precious commodity in the survival situation, your rations may not be enough to reverse the acute stages of dehydration. It is vital to understand the dehydration process and learn what preventive actions can be taken to help slow down the process.

Prevention

- When in conditions where dehydration may occur and water is available, drink as much water as possible.
- Unless there is an ample supply of water, avoid the intake of salt. Your body will regulate your level of salt by excreting the proper amount in your sweat. Excess salt will cause the loss of precious body fluids in the form of sweat.

- Do not smoke because it will increase your need for water.

- No alcohol. Alcohol will not fulfill your body's need for water, and may result in vomiting, thus losing precious fluids.

- Minimize food intake, relative to the amount of water available. In situations where food is available, but water isn't, you should avoid the intake of food. The digestion of food, and particularly carbohydrates, requires water. In fact, you would probably succumb to a lack of water long before you would die from starvation.

- In arctic areas, never eat snow directly. The body must expend energy and moisture to melt snow that you have eaten. You must melt the snow before consuming it.

- Ration your sweat. In situations where water is not available in any significant quantity, the only way to conserve what body fluids you do have is to control and minimize the amount that you perspire.

- In hot climates minimize your activities during the hot periods of the day. Rowing, working, and any strenuous activities should be saved for the cooler periods of the day or for night. The less sweat your body uses to cool itself, the more moisture your body will retain. Work at a slow pace if work is necessary during the day.

- Create some shade and remain under it as much as possible. Use a canopy, tarp, a hat, or even your clothes to construct a sun barrier.

- Wear protective clothing such as a long sleeve shirt, trousers, or a hat. This traps the perspiration and slows down its evaporation, which gives you the fullest cooling effect. This principle is illustrated in desert areas, for example, where desert tribesmen cover themselves completely.

- In warm areas where hypothermia is not an immediate threat, saturate your clothing with sea water. This will increase the cooling effect to some degree.

- Be prepared to recognize the imaginings and hallucinations that come with acute stages of dehydration. Castaways have been known to become irrational and delirious and drink anything in their desperate attempt to slake their thirst.

- Never under any circumstances drink urine or straight sea water! Both urine and seawater have an extremely heavy salt content. Body fluids must be used to flush the salt out of the kidneys, and this process speeds up the dehydration process considerably.

Note: Some castaways have successfully reported mixing seawater with their water stores in closely controlled proportions (such as 1 part seawater to 2 parts fresh water). A noted marine researcher, Dr. Alain Bombard, purports to have survived for 65 days in a raft by mixing seawater with fresh water, as well as obtaining liquids from fish. However, this is a controversial issue, and most experts still advise castaways against the ingestion of seawater in any form whatsoever.

6
Navigation

NAVIGATION IN A SURVIVAL CRAFT IS NOT PRE-cise. First, the survival raft is designed to stay afloat rather than sail. You are not, however, completely at the mercy of the elements, since you can influence, to some degree, the effect of wind and current on your raft.

Knowledge of your position can help you make decisions concerning choice and plan of action. Your position, once known, can aid you in finding the distance and direction to land, to a shipping lane, or perhaps to an area of greater rainfall. Determining your position can also help you make decisions concerning rations and may also favorably influence mental attitudes, if for no other reason than simply giving you something to do to improve your situation.

POSITION PLOTTING PROCEDURE

If you are lucky you had the time and presence to grab your sextant and tables and bring them along in the raft. If not, or if you don't know how to work the sextant, the following tables and simple procedures will allow you to ascertain a position within ½ degree (30 nautical miles) and which, if plotted daily, will show you your progress and direction.

One added advantage of the following method of celestial navigation is that you are not dependent upon an assumed position, nor must you plot azimuths or distances. You have, in effect, reduced your chances for error.

To plot your position, you must first determine your latitude and longitude.

Latitude is the measurement, in degrees, of the distance north and south of the equator. New York is approximately 40 degrees north in latitude. Sydney Australia's latitude is about 34 degrees south.

Longitude is the measurement, in degrees, that you are east or west of Greenwich, England. (A reference point represented by an imaginary vertical line bisecting Greenwich, England). Los Angeles' longitude is about 120 degrees west. Paris is about 2 degrees east.

Once you establish these approximate values by using the following method you can plot a daily position and course on a chart and determine the distance and direction you have traveled.

DETERMINING YOUR LATITUDE

When you know the day's date and are able to calculate the length of the day within one minute, you will be able to determine your latitude. (Providing you are at a latitude between 60 degrees north and 60 degrees south. Another exception is between the days of March 11 and 13 and from September 13 through October 2, at which periods the day's length is almost exactly the same at all latitudes.)

- With your watch, time the exact length of the day from the moment the sun first appears on the horizon (east) to the exact instant it disappears on the western horizon. This means the instant the top of the sun first appears on the horizon to the exact instant the top of the sun disappears below the horizon. (Sometimes marked by a green flash caused by atmospheric refraction.)

- Follow the instructions on the nomogram (Fig. 6-1) for calculating your latitude.

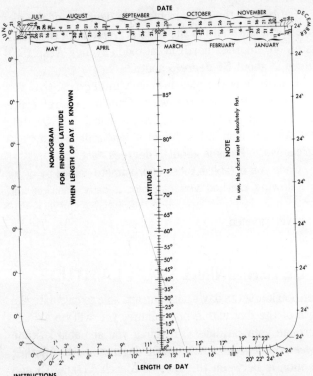

INSTRUCTIONS

To find your latitude:

In Northern Latitudes:

1. Find length of the day from the instant the top of the sun appears above the ocean horizon to the instant it disappears below the horizon. This instant is often marked by a green flash.

2. Lay a straight edge or stretch across the Nomogram, connecting the observed length of the day on the Length of Day Scale with the date on the Date Scale.

3. Read your latitude on the Latitude Scale.

EXAMPLE: On August 20, observed length of the day is 13 hours and 54 minutes. Latitude is 45°30'N.

In Southern Latitudes:

Add six months to the date and proceed as in northern latitudes.

EXAMPLE: On 11 May observed length of day is 10 hours and 4 minutes. Adding 6 months gives 11 November. Latitude is 41°30'S.

Fig. 6-1 Nomogram.

DETERMINING YOUR LONGITUDE FROM APPARENT NOON

- To find your longitude you need to know the rate at which your watch gains or loses time and the time that you last set your watch.

Example:

Your watch gains 1 minute per day.
You last set your watch 4 days ago.
Your watch indicates 12:28 a.m.

        12:28
    minus   4
    equals 12:24
    Corrected or "real" time is 12:24.

- Convert to military time: Convert time to 24 hour periods. i.e., 11:00 a.m. is 1100; 1:00 p.m. is 1300; 10:00 p.m. is 2200, and so on.
- Determine apparent local noon: Simply divide the total hours and minutes of the day by 2. Noon is exactly half way between sunrise and sunset.
- Convert local noon to Greenwich time. To do this refer to the World Time Zone (Fig. 6-2). Find the appropriate time zone and correct your local apparent noon time by adding or subtracting the indicated hours on the bottom of the table. For example: You are located on the eastern coast of Florida so your time correction would be +5 hours.

> Local adjusted noon: 12:24
> correction plus   ± 5:00
> Greenwich time of
> local apparent noon. 17:24

- Adjust time of local apparent noon: Refer to the Date

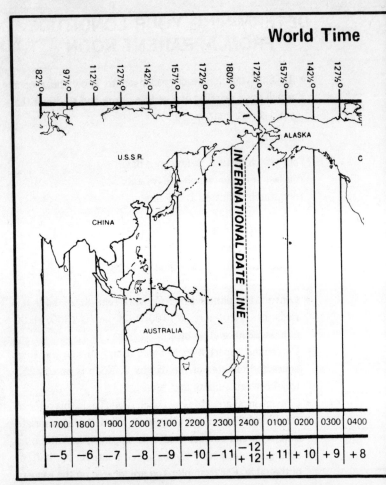

Fig. 6-2 World Time Zone Chart.

Time Equation chart (Table 6-1) for correction of the time that the observed sun is ahead or behind of the "mean" sun. (The observed sun changes its angular rate of travel according to the seasons. For this reason, astronomers invented the "mean" sun which moves along the equator at a constant rate, 15 degrees per hour.)

Zone Chart

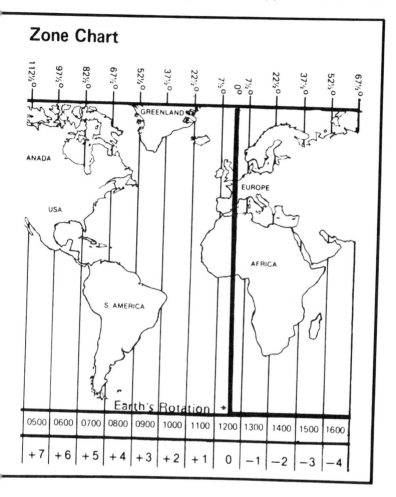

0500	0600	0700	0800	0900	1000	1100	1200	1300	1400	1500	1600
+7	+6	+5	+4	+3	+2	+1	0	−1	−2	−3	−4

Example:

Greenwich time of local noon: 17:24
date adjustment for August 29 minus   01 minute
equated Greenwich time
of apparent noon. 17:23

- Determine position: Calculate the difference between Greenwich noon and the "equated" Greenwich time of local apparent noon:

Table 6-1. Date-Time Equation
Chart for Longitude Determination

Date		Eq. of Time*	Date		Eq. of Time*
Jan.	1	−3.5 min.	Aug.	4	−6.0 min.
	2	−4.0		12	−5.0
	4	−5.0		17	−4.0
	7	−6.0		22	−3.0
	9	−7.0		26	−2.0
	12	−8.0		29	−1.0
	14	−9.0	Sept.	1	0.0
	17	−10.0		5	+1.0
	20	−11.0		8	+2.0
	24	−12.0		10	+3.0
	28	−13.0		13	+4.0
Feb.	4	−14.0		16	+5.0
	13	−14.3		19	+6.0
	19	−14.0		22	+7.0
	28	−13.0		25	+8.0
				28	+9.0
Mar.	4	−12.0			
	8	−11.0	Oct.	1	+10.0
	12	−10.0		4	+11.0
	16	−9.0		7	+12.0
	19	−8.0		11	+13.0
	22	−7.0		15	+14.0
	26	−6.0		20	+15.0
	29	−5.0		27	+16.0
Apr.	1	−4.0	Nov.	4	+16.4
	5	−3.0		11	+16.0
	8	−2.0		17	+15.0
	12	−1.0		22	+14.0
	16	0.0		25	+13.0
	20	+1.0		28	+12.0
	25	+2.0	Dec.	1	+11.0
May	2	+3.0		4	+10.0
	14	+3.8		6	+9.0
	28	+3.0		9	+8.0
				11	+7.0
June	4	+2.0		13	+6.0
	9	+1.0		15	+5.0
	14	0.0		17	+4.0

Date	Eq. of Time*	Date	Eq. of Time*
19		19	+3.0
23	−1.0	21	+2.0
28	−2.0	23	+1.0
	−3.0	25	0.0
July 3	−4.0	27	−1.0
9	−5.0	29	−2.0
18	−6.0	31	−3.0
27	−6.6		

*Add plus to time and subtract from time to get apparent time.

Example:

Greenwich time of apparent noon (equated):	17:23
Greenwich noon is: minus	−12:00
difference in time is.	5:23

• Calculate position: To establish how many degrees you are from Greenwich England you must only compute the following:

one hour equals 15 degrees of longitude
four minutes equals 1 degree of longitude
difference in time is 5 hours:

5 hours × 15 degrees equals	75 degrees
23 min divided by 4 equals	5.75 minutes
added together equals	80.75 degrees

Your position is *80 degrees 45 minutes* west longitude. *Note:* Since there are 60 longitude "minutes" in a longitude "degree," do not confuse navigation "minutes" with watch or clock minutes.

If you had to add hours to Greenwich time during your time zone correction then you are west of Greenwich. If you had subtracted hours, then you are east of Greenwich.

Note: If your watch has been set to daylight savings time, your conversion to GMT (Greenwich Mean Time) will be one hour less than from the time on the chart. (In the example above you would add only four hours, not five.)

7

Operational
Survival Skills

ABANDONING SHIP

The decision of whether or not to abandon ship is a serious one that is, in the majority of cases, dictated by circumstance and necessity. There are really only two situations in which it is absolutely necessary to abandon ship: an uncontrollable fire aboard that threatens both lives and the vessel; or a capsizing of or other damage to the vessel that causes it to sink.

In all other situations it is probably best to stay with the parent craft as long as possible. Too often, a panicked crew has taken to the life raft and perished while the unattended parent vessel has weathered the storm still afloat and intact. Tragic incidents of this type have been documented in all areas of boating — from the weekender, to the blue water cruiser, and even to the professional racer. "Never leave your ship until it leaves you" is an old rule that could have saved lives in numerous situations if it had only been adhered to.

Preparing to Abandon

Proper planning will give you the confidence and the tools with which to survive an open water survival situation. Knowing that you can survive in a raft is important, but don't be too hasty in making the decision to abandon ship. You must first decide whether to use the precious minutes available to attempt repairs to a damaged hull (by using a "collision mat" or a plug) or whether to begin gathering survival equipment. With available tools you may be able to stop the water inlet or at least keep the hull afloat a little longer, allowing you time to gather more equipment, send another SOS, and provide a better visual target for rescue.

Flotation Bags. The ideal method of protecting your vessel in the event of a sinking is to have flotation bags to keep the vessel afloat. These bags are strategically stored inside the vessel, ready for rapid deployment in the event of an emergency. Vessel flotation bags can also be improvised by using the inner tubes of large, heavy equipment tires connected to a rapid inflation mechanism. When inflated, the bags should fill the inside of the vessel and keep it afloat.

Locating a Leak. It may be easier to find the leak in a hull by feeling for it rather than by trying to detect it visually. Check under piles of supplies, for example, and feel around with your hands in inaccessible corners and crevices. Remember, however, that once a leak is below the waterline it will be very difficult to locate.

If you find a hole, try to contain it by cutting up light sails and filling the hole, or by wrapping the exterior of the hull with a sail or collision mat. A sail placed on the outside of the hull covering a hole will be held in place by the pressure of the water (Fig. 7-1).

External wrapping of the hull with a sail or collision mat over a hole that is aft of admidships may prove ineffective, since the prop and rudder will most likely prevent an effective seal.

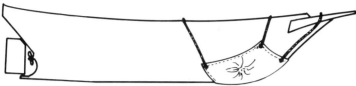

Fig. 7-1 Method of improvising a collision mat to plug a hole, using a sail.

While it is important to try to locate the leak, with the hope of perhaps repairing it, don't let the search for a leak delay or keep you from pumping water or preparing for abandoning ship.

Bailing and Pumping. Don't stop bailing or pumping, because every amount of water expelled from the boat converts into extra time afloat for other efforts. Buckets may be necessary, regardless of the size of the bilge pump.

Abandoning Ship. Once the decision is made to abandon ship, your chance of survival will be influenced by how you accomplish this and what you take with you. Boats have been known to sink in a matter of minutes, barely allowing time to get the life raft overboard. Consequently, it is not difficult to understand the wisdom of having a grab bag of supplies prepared and stored in an easily accessible place in the event of an emergency.

ABANDON SHIP PROCEDURES

• Discuss with the crew procedures for abandoning ship, including delegation of responsibilities, location of vital survival stores, and life raft launching procedures. The onset of an emergency situation is no time to acquire these skills; they should be drilled and practiced before an emergency. The following are the procedures to follow when abandoning ship:

- Don a PFD.
- Assess damage to the boat, and attempt to repair it if practical.

- Send an SOS stating position and situation.
- Launch the life raft. Use the leeward side so that the parent vessel will block any rough seas and weather and so that any flotsam will drift toward you for salvage after the vessel sinks. Don't wait until the last minute to inflate your life raft system. If a malfunction occurs in the automatic inflation mechanism additional time will be required for manual inflations.
- Station one person at the painter that connects the raft to the boat, with knife in hand prepared to cut the line.
- Transfer all supplies to the raft in order of their importance, which should already have been predetermined.
- Position the life raft at a safe distance from the parent vessel, but keep it in sight to make sure that the vessel actually sinks.
- Salvage anything and everything remotely usable that may be floating around you. Make sure you don't bring aboard anything that may threaten the life raft with sharp edges or points.
- Tie together all rafts at a safe distance. Once the currents and winds take over, you may never again be close enough to do this.
- Check the life raft, bailing out water or making any repairs if necessary.
- Assess the physical condition of the crew and treat all injuries immediately.
- Activate the EPIRB, if applicable.
- Inventory your survival stores, and log pertinent information.
- Ration the food, and give the crew a ration of water.
- Raise the canopy.

LAUNCHING THE LIFE RAFT

Launching

Launching is any means of getting the life raft or boat over the side and floating while it is still secured to the parent craft by a line. The mistake of forgetting to secure the bitter end of the line that is attached to the life raft or dinghy is a common, but very serious one. In the confusion surrounding an emergency situation, the possibility of a panicked crew member throwing the life raft overboard without an attached line is very real. This type of a mistake happens frequently with anchors, even in normal anchoring procedures. It is advisable to secure a lengthy line from the raft to the boat while the raft is stowed on deck. Tie the line in such a manner that the life raft can be launched and the line payed out without having to be untied or attended to.

CO₂ Inflation

Once the life raft container is over the side, a sharp "tug" on the line or painter will activate the carbon dioxide inflation system and at the same time provide a secured line to the boat. This not only prevents the inflated raft from drifting away (especially in high winds) but allows you to concentrate on other activities, such as collecting and loading valuable gear.

Painter

The object is to launch, inflate, and board the raft, and then cut the painter loose before the parent craft sinks. Should the parent craft be sinking too fast, you may have time only to launch the life raft and abandon ship into the water. If this happens, the connecting line between the raft and the parent craft must be severed, to ensure that the life raft does not go down with the ship.

BOARDING THE RAFT

If at all possible, board the raft from the parent craft to avoid getting wet. If a "water boarding" must be used, let the strongest person climb into the raft first so that he can aid the others in boarding.

To help an injured or exhausted crew member aboard, grab onto the person from behind, gripping him under the shoulders or armpits, and then hoist him upward rather than to try and push or pull him aboard (Fig. 7-2).

Discuss procedure and duties for righting an overturned raft before you find yourself in that situation! Floating in the water with a capsized raft in heavy seas and strong winds is not time to learn how to do it!

AFLOAT IN THE LIFE RAFT

Feelings of panic, despair, and hopelessness can easily surface while afloat in a life raft. The disappointment following the sighting of a ship or plane that doesn't see you, for example, can be devastating. Because of the shock, both mentally and physically, of being stranded in a survival situation is acute, it is advisable to begin delegating duties, establishing goals, and setting up routines and schedules immediately.

It is your attitude, faith, and perseverance that are key ingredients in your ability to survive. The will to survive is your strongest tool. It has been proven over and over again that positive thinking and positive actions are the absolute keys to coping with even the most seemingly hopeless of situations.

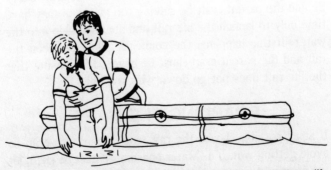

Fig. 7-2 The correct way to assist another person boarding a life raft.

Delegating Duties

The presence of an officer or captain on board the survival craft will determine who is in charge. If, however, for any reason that person chooses not to retain command, it is important that some person assume the role of leader. Whoever the leader may be, his rank must be respected and supported.

The person in charge should delegate duties to ensure that important tasks are carried out and that there is no duplication of work. Chores should begin immediately.

Delegating Responsibilities

- Assess the situation. Determine the condition of the raft and the condition of the survivors (physical and mental). Delegate responsibilities accordingly.
- Keep every crew member abreast of the situation and developments. Arrange a daily meeting to discuss and update the situation to determine what must be accomplished during the day and by whom. This promotes good morale as well as a feeling of unity.
- Convey a feeling of acceptance to each of the crew members, especially the disabled or ill. Be certain that every crew member feels that he or she is contributing to the survival group and is vital in some way, no matter how trivial it may actually be.
- Avoid dissention at all costs.

Establish Goals

Establishing goals, whether they are long-term or short-term goals, will contribute to positive actions and positive thinking. Focusing on goals will also help you maintain a stable mental and physical condition, which is essential to your survival. Establishing goals will also ensure that the vital tasks of obtaining and rationing food and water are based on extended goals.

You have a much better chance of surviving if you mentally prepare yourself for surviving the longest possible time afloat. It is a good idea to think of rescue as a welcome interruption to a directed voyage toward landfall, rather than placing all your hope on a chance rescue.

Establish Routines

Just as setting a goal is vital and important to the overall well-being of the castaway, so is the task of setting up daily routines or schedules. Once established, strictly adhere to the schedule.

An established routine will give relief and purpose to the situation, will help pass time, will occupy the minds of the crew, and will provide something to look forward to. More importantly, it will assure that certain necessary duties are carried out.

• Establishing a routine of daily events on the life raft lends a feeling of "normalcy" to an otherwise alien and perilous situation. Establishing routines and schedules will also aid morale. Meals, for instance, should be eaten at set times only. This helps give reference to passing time, as well as something to look forward to. Allocate a certain time each day for conversation or games. Even the detailed daydreaming descriptions of food or other fantasies can support the will to live, and is a good example of a positive activity that may be included in a daily routine.

THE LIFE RAFT ROUTINE

The following is a list of basic duties and routines which, if scheduled and performed, can enhance the morale of the group and will help maximize the chances of a successful survival.

Inventory. Itemize and list all stores, such as water, flares, fish hooks, and so on. It is best to itemize supplies by examining them carefully one at a time, rather than all at once. This will minimize the loss of unsecured items overboard in the event of a sudden movement by a crew member or even an unexpected capsizing.

Rations. Divide and list the rationing amounts. Plan for the longest period of deprivation. Refrain from drinking or eating anything for the first 24 hours. This will activate the "water-saving" capabilities of your body. *Note:* When drinking your water ration, sip it slowly and let it spread throughout your mouth before swallowing. This has a positive psychological effect in cases of water deprivation.

Compile a Log. Record the last "fix" (longitude/latitude), last transmission, course, present wind direction, swell direction, time of sinking, etc. If possible, continue the log for the duration of the survival situation.

Inspections. Make routine inspections to avoid unnecessary trouble or repairs that result from neglect. Establish a schedule of inspections:

- All areas of strain or chafe and places where towing lines are attached should be checked regularly.
- Lines, sea anchors, knots, leaks, repairs, and bailing chores must be attended to regularly.
- Periodically assess the condition of injured crew members, and attend to their needs accordingly.
- Inspect the pressure of the buoyancy chambers. On hot days, as in the tropics, it may be necessary to release some air to compensate for expanding hot air. The reverse will hold true in cold weather areas.

Lookouts. Watches or lookouts should begin immediately to maximize the chance of being detected or of sighting land. This also helps to establish a good routine for the duration of the time afloat.

Length of Watch. Depending on the situation and the number of crew available, a two-hour watch is a good maximum. If the crew is debilitated from exposure or dehydration, or, if heavy work such as bailing or rowing is necessary, then a much shorter watch period would be in order.

Schedules. Schedule each person for his same watch time each day or night. This is so that any changes in conditions such as wind or swell direction, rising stars, etc. will be more easily detected.

Eyestrain. While on watch, the lookout must protect himself against eyestrain. Extreme cases of eyestrain can result in temporary blindness, which can be brought on by prolonged exposure to such elements as snow, ice, or bright sunlight. Eyeshades or sunglasses should be worn and can be easily improvised if necessary.

Attend to Crew. The lookout person must also be attentive to his companions and to the valuable stores on board. He should make certain that all stores remain in secured, safe positions and that the injured are checked upon regularly. He should be able to recognize the warning symptoms of hypothermia in a crew member, and must see that no one is exposed either to sunburn or frostbite, and that no one is trailing a hand or foot in the water.

False Alarms. Since the object of a lookout is to sight land or a rescue vessel, it is wise to discuss the ramifications of a false alarm on the morale of a distressed crew. The accidental raising of hopes by a premature "yell" of sighting land or a ship can have serious effects of despair on the exhausted crew. First summon the leader to verify any indications of landfall or rescue before alerting the entire crew.

Miscellaneous Life Raft Skills

Hygiene. Keep the raft's interior as dry as possible. This promotes good hygiene and helps to prevent exposure related problems (immersion foot, salt water boils, hypothermia, etc.)

Avoiding Mistakes. When passing important rations or tools, use a verbal communication system. For example, when handing a sextant to someone, before you let go, ask: "Sextant secure?" and wait to hear "sextant is secure" before you release it.

•   **Righting the Raft.** You should expect and be prepared for a capsizing. Being prepared includes lashing and securing your stores as well as mentally going over the procedures and educating the rest of the crew in their duties. Do this now, before you experience a capsizing and the chaos that goes with it (Fig. 7-3).

Fishing Tips
Fishing line:

• Never tie a fishing line directly to the raft unless you are capable of quickly cutting it.
• If necessary, fishing line can be fashioned out of wire or unraveled rope.

   Bait. Try to make the bait appear natural. Conceal it if possible and jiggle it slowly to make it appear alive.

   Night Fishing. The use of any type of light at night will often attract fish. A torch, flashlight, or even the moon's reflection through a mirror will accomplish this.

   Gaff Hook. The most effective fishing technique may be using the gaff hook. Its use has been documented in several stores of survival, apparently due to the frequent appearance of surface fish.

Fig. 7-3 The proper way to right a life raft with the aid of the wind.

EMPLOYING THE SEA ANCHOR

One of the principal functions of a sea anchor (or drogue) is to provide stability in a rough or heavy sea. Because a raft floats on the water rather than in the water, it is susceptible to high winds. By trailing a sea anchor you can minimize the possibility of capsizing in high winds or heavy seas. The sea anchor will slow down the drift of the raft, which may be advantageous if you have sent an SOS transmission and want to remain close to the area of the transmission or the capsizing.

The principle involved in using a sea anchor is to create a "drag" effect that will:

- Slow down the drift of the raft
- Give you direction and control
- Stabilize the raft
- Minimize capsizing

Often a sea anchor will continually spin or twist, causing the line to unravel or part. A swivel shackle, if available, can be added to prevent this (Fig. 7-4).

Improvising a sea anchor is easy if a sturdy line is available, as well as anything that will create a drag when towed. For example, oil skins, cloths, or cans could be used (Fig. 7-5).

Position the sea anchor over the stern so that it is in

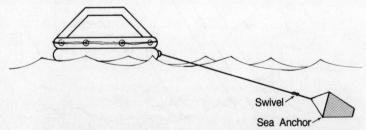

Swivel

Sea Anchor

Fig. 7-4 The proper deployment of a sea anchor will give directional stability to a life raft.

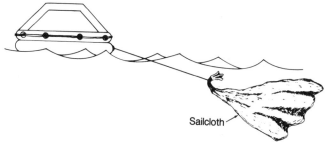

Sailcloth

Fig. 7-5 One method of improvising a sea anchor is by using a large piece of canvas or any other sturdy material available.

the trough of the wave when your raft is on the wave's crest. Use a liberal amount of line and adjust it constantly in order to keep a strain on the line.

TO STAY PUT OR TRAVEL

The choice of whether to stay put or to travel in the life raft is a controversial one. Each survival situation is unique, and this decision can be made by evaluating the conditions in force. Even then you have no guarantee which decision is best since you have no way of foreseeing factors of chance. There are, however, several points you should consider in making your choice.

Deciding to Travel

SOS. If an SOS transmission was *never* sent, it may be that no one is aware of your situation or whereabouts. In this case, it may *not* be to your advantage to remain in the same area.

Knowledge. If you know where you are, and know where land is located or where there might be a shipping lane, then it may be advisable to try and reach them.

Near Land. If you definitely know that you are near land, and that you won't exhaust yourself by fighting an "up-hill" battle against the elements, then it would be advisable to travel.

Goal. If it is deemed most advisable to travel, whether it be to reach a landfall, shipping lane, or an area with greater rainfall, you would be taking a positive action to try to improve your situation. This promotes a feeling of accomplishment.

Mode of Travel. If you have a suitable craft for sailing (such as a sailing dinghy), or are in strong currents, or perhaps have good navigation gear, then the best decision may be to direct your efforts toward a destination.

Landfall. Remember: trying to navigate and locate a 2-mile-long, flat island in a raft may be too much to ask for. If you are aware of your position and have a choice of more than one landfall, choose the larger landfall.

Deciding Not to Travel

SOS. If you sent an SOS stating position you might want to wait and remain as near as possible to the last point of transmission.

SOS Acknowledged. If your SOS was acknowledged, it is advisable to remain as close as possible to your stated position for a reasonable period of time.

Conserving Energy. If you are totally unsure of your whereabouts, then it is usually better to stay put and use your energies for other activities. Moving consumes energy that is perhaps better saved for the basic task of living and trying to survive in the life raft.

LANDFALL

Once you have determined that setting out for landfall is your best course of action, the following section will provide you with specific information to help you locate, evaluate, and effect a successful landing. Because of the wide range of geographic variables that differ from one situation to another, evaluate the following information in terms of your own circumstances.

Locating A Landfall

Any of the following conditions may be an indication of a landfall:

Greenish Tint in the Sky. A tropical island can sometimes be detected by a greenish tint in the sky. This is caused by light reflections emanating from shallow lagoons and bays surrounding the island.

Lighter Colored Water. Deep water is prominantly dark green or dark blue. A significant lightening of the ocean water around you may indicate shallow water, which could signal the closeness of land.

Smells. Be aware of any smells that may come from a nearby landmass. An inhabited or heavily vegetated island might produce strong odors or scents. Anything from campfires, to flowers, to swamps, to spoiled fish can give off a smell. If you are located downwind, you may be able to detect such smells from a nearby landmass.

Sound of Surf. The sound of breaking surf may indicate a shallow reef surrounding an island, or will signal the actual shore itself. In the case of reduced visibility from dense fog, mist, or rain, the roar of the surf can be heard long before breaking surf can be spotted.

Cloud Reflections. In the arctic regions, snow covered land areas, or large ice fields are often indicated by light-colored reflections on clouds. This is markedly different from the normal darkish gray reflections caused by open ocean.

Birds. The continual cries of marine birds coming from one direction may indicate their roosting place on a nearby island or coastal area. Also, the sighting of birds flying overhead may indicate the direction of land.

Mirages. Mirages are a real phenomenon in a survival situation, and are quite common in tropical environments, especially during the middle of the day. A mirage may change appearance and height while being viewed, and can also shimmer and disappear. Beware of mistaking a mirage for a landfall.

Choosing a Landfall

Remember: Having reached or sighted land does not necessarily guarantee the end of the survival ordeal.

Bear in mind that a large island, once sighted, might still be another 5 to 6 days away. Be prudent with your rations.

One of the most difficult decisions a survivor might face will be the decision to pass by a landfall. Adverse conditions might necessitate having to pass by a landfall because:

- Landing on a barren island that won't sustain life may only worsen your situation and might even damage your life raft in the process.
- Treacherous surf or steep cliffs that would endanger life and limb in the landing process should also be avoided. (Remember, the dehydrated castaway may not be capable of walking, let alone swimming.)
- If the decision is made to pass by the landfall, you may have to convince a desperate or less experienced crew to agree with you.

Evaluating a Landfall

Deciding to attempt a landfall, as well as choosing the method and location, calls for serious evaluation. To be successful, you must complete the landing and survive it.

Landing at Night. If possible, never attempt a landfall at night. Wait for daylight to see the surf or reef lines or any other potential dangers.

Coral Reefs. Try to avoid landing near coral reefs. The razor sharp coral can shred your skin, as well as the life raft. Often the distance from the sandy shore of a tropical island to the end of the shallow reef is considerable.

Rivers. On islands fringed by coral reefs it is best to seek the outlet of a river. Coral cannot thrive in fresh water, and consequently, wherever there is a fresh water river emptying into the ocean there will be an opening through the coral reef.

Exploding Waves. Try to avoid places where the waves explode with high spray and white water. This usually indicates that the waves are breaking on shallow reefs, rocky shores, or vertical cliffs.

Your Physical Condition. Consider the physical stamina and condition of yourself and your crew. Dehydration, prolonged periods of sitting without exercise, and exposure to the elements are all extremely debilitating.

Wave Conditions. The size of the surf on the lee side of an island is usually smaller than on the windward side, so this may be your best place to land.

Remember that from the ocean and from your raft, you can only see the smooth "backs" of the waves, which can be very misleading as to their actual size. Wave size is sometimes smaller during ebb tide.

Directional Control. When drifting toward land, utilize any directional control you have as quickly as possible, before your control of direction is lost to prevailing winds, currents, or wave patterns.

Land Travel. Remember that it is easier for an exhausted or injured survivor to travel by way of raft on the ocean along the coast than to hike over mountains or other rugged terrain.

PREPARING TO LAND

Once you decide to land you must do everything you can to make the landing operation as safe as possible.

- Wear your PFD (personal flotation jacket) if you have one.
- Wear clothing and shoes, if possible, to protect you from the rocks and coral. (Make sure they won't weigh you down too much in the event that you are capsized and have to swim.)
- Portion out an extra ration of water to provide additional

nourishment and also lessen the amount of water that may be lost overboard.

- Use a sea anchor. A sea anchor is extremely important when surf is present to minimize the chance of capsizing. The purpose of a sea anchor, when adjusted properly, is to keep the raft in the trough and off the crest of the waves. If a proper sea anchor is not available, now would be a good time to improvise one, even at the expense of some valuable clothing.

- Create ballast and greater buoyancy by filling the raft with sea water (weather permitting) and by deflating the lower tube or chamber of the raft to produce a sluggish effect. This will also help minimize capsizing. (Remember, rafts that have deep ballast pockets may encounter problems when negotiating shallow reefs.)

- Sit low in the raft to place the center of gravity as low as possible. If you are going to lay down, lay on your side to avoid back injuries from bumping against rocks or coral, with your feet forward (toward shore).

- Have the stronger survivors float outside the raft, if the raft is dangerously overcrowded, by holding onto the grommeted safety line that is attached to the outside of the raft. This will add more ballast to the raft, and may produce some additional control.

- Remove the canopy to make escape easier in the event of a capsizing.

Effecting the Landing

Before you attempt the landing, study the waves breaking on shore. Groups of waves approach shore in regular cycles. These cycles will consist of sets of large waves followed by small waves. The wave sets typically run from five to nine waves, followed by a lull. Time the sets, and effect your landing during the time of minimum wave action.

Keep in mind that it will be very difficult to prevent capsizing if the waves are sizable. Should the raft capsize:

- Try to stay with it. Although you run the risk of being hindered or struck by the raft, you have a greater chance of surviving by holding on to it. The raft should eventually carry you toward shore.

- Position yourself when you are in the water so that you are on the "seaward side" of the raft. This will afford you the protection of the raft itself.

- Should you find yourself adrift alone in pounding surf, roll up into a ball and try to roll with the waves. Keep your life jacket on. It is never a good idea to shed your life jacket to try to swim or dive under the waves.

- Don't try to swim through seaweed, but simply crawl over it using an overhand motion.

Controlling the Life Raft

Directional control of an inflatable life raft is minimal at best, but it can be improved by using a sea anchor. A sea anchor will help to prevent the raft from spinning, which in turn will help reduce the possibility of sea sickness. Sea anchors can also be used with a rigid type craft to function in the same capacity, for the same reasons, and in addition will help give the bow of the boat direction.

Some degree of control can be effected by opening the canopy "door" of the raft. This can to some extent create a "sail" (or more precisely a wind pocket) that can increase the raft's downwind travel. This may also provide a more comfortable ride if used in conjunction with prevailing winds and waves. It may, however, be impossible to do this in rough or heavy seas.

Use the ocean currents or wind direction to gain some control. A sea anchor can help you take advantage of the currents. Use favorable wind direction by providing as large a mass as possible on the ocean surface. This can be accomplished by creating a sail or perhaps just sitting up as high as possible to provide more surface to the wind.

• WATER: THE LIFE SOURCE

In most ocean survival ordeals, the predominant factor governing survival is the ability to obtain fresh water. Water is essential to survival, and is far more necessary than food. In fact, it is possible to live for weeks on water alone, while existence without it leads to delirium in a few days' time.

Medical authorities have established that a minimum of one pint of water per day is sufficient for one person to exist. The actual amount, however, may vary from one individual to another and also might be affected by factors such as: the climate (air temperature and humidity), the conservation of body fluids, exposure to the elements, physical exertion, and your individual resistance.

SURVIVAL WATER SOURCES

Solar Still. The solar still was developed primarily for use in survival kits for naval aviators in time of war and provides an excellent source of potable water for the castaway. When deflated, the solar still measures about 6″×6″×2″ and is easily stored. When inflated, the 24″ diameter ball is capable of collecting more than a quart of fresh water per day in temperate climates with sunshine. Water is produced through the principle of condensation (Fig. 7-6).

Solar stills are reusable, require no chemicals, and are capable of producing some amount of water even on slightly overcast days. Since a solar still requires sunshine to produce water, it is of course restricted to daytime use. Its ability to produce water on heavy, overcast days and in rough seas is impaired.

Desalinization Kits. You can use desalinization kits both day or night for converting sea water into potable water. When applied to one pint of salt water, the desalting briquet will precipitate the salt, which is then removed by a filter bag. The water is usually acrid and discolored,

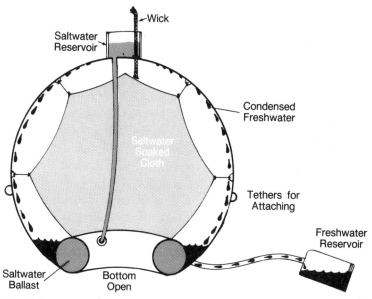

Fig. 7-6 Solar Still.

but when prepared according to instructions, it is safe for consumption.

For storage economy, it is estimated that each de-salting kit can produce about seven times the amount of fresh water that could be stored in the same space. An advantage of the desalinization kit is that it can be used to produce potable water when conditions restrict the use of the solar still.

Rain Water. Without the aid of water producing devices, such as solar stills or a desalinization kit, your only source of fresh water will be from the sky. Water is also available through moisture in the air (dew, condensation, frost), but rain comprises the only viable immediate source.

A rain catchment device can be improvised from your life raft canopy, sails, clothing, or any such surface. Or, a tarp included specifically for funneling water may be included in your survival provisions.

It is critical to collect rainwater as efficiently as possible. Because of the inconsistency of rainfall in many areas, you will not be able to count on rain to fulfill your water needs at regular intervals. You must instead maximize the amount of water that you can collect and store from any one rainfall to hold you through dry periods of no rain.

Dew and Condensation. Collection of condensation from surfaces that are free of salt can yield fair amounts of potable water. Condensation forms occasionally and, if collected with clean materials, can provide precious water for the castaway.

Ice. Once melted, ice is an alternative source of potable water. It should never be consumed directly because it requires vital body heat and fluids to melt it internally. (*Note:* For information on how to distinguish salt-laden ice from freshwater ice, see Chapter 9).

Fish. In times of acute water shortage, fluids can be obtained from the blood and body fluids of fish. Separate the vertebrae or break the backbone and drink the spinal fluid. The entire fish can also be tightly squeezed in a thin cloth, and the resulting fluids consumed. Some types of fish have large eyes that yield sizable amounts of fluid.

Blood. The blood of birds and sea turtles is drinkable, providing both nourishment and fluids.

Storage

To store fresh water in a life raft, you need containers that won't break or cut the raft fabric. They should be resealable and easily retrievable in the event of a capsize. Plastic containers serve the purpose very well. If filled ¾ full, plastic containers will float and are resealable. It is best to store plastic jugs out of the sun.

Water provisions stored in tin cans for prolonged periods may turn bad and become undrinkable. A viable alternative is to purchase club soda or mineral water in aluminum or plastic containers. This makes periodic updating of your water provisions very convenient since these items are widely available.

WATER SKILLS

Thirst. Be aware that thirst is not always an accurate indicator of the body's need for water. Physical exertion in colder climates, for example, can produce fluid loss through sweat, even though the body may not signal its need for water by making your feel thirsty. Nevertheless, the need for water is still present.

Food Intake. Food intake also greatly increases the need for water. Water, in the form of gastric juices, is required to digest and assimilate food. Therefore, when water is not available, avoid all intake of food, since precious body fluids will be used up in the digestive process.

Water Requirement. A minimum of one pint of water per day is sufficient for one person to exist; the rationing of any less than one pint of water a day can severely debilitate the castaway, defeating the purpose of stretching the water supply.

Remember that survival requires a coherent state of mind and rational actions. There are records of survivors lasting as long as seven days on less than a pint of water a day. But individual resistance varies greatly and is influenced by environmental conditions.

COLLECTING WATER

If you have a solar still, deploy it as soon as weather permits. Take advantage of all fair weather periods, and continually top off your water supplies as well as your body's supply. Remember these critical points involved in catching rainwater:

- Ensure that it is not contaminated from any surface you are using to funnel and catch it.
- Catch as much as possible when the opportunity arises.

The person on watch should always keep an eye out for the appearance of potential rain clouds. A sudden cloud burst may leave you with next to nothing if you are not prepared to catch the rain. Since most survival craft cannot be steered or propelled, you must take advantage of the sudden arrival of a rain cloud.

Procedures

- Plan ahead. Prerig a catchment, canopy, or runoff of some design so that it can be set up quickly and easily. Be prepared.
- When the possibility of rain is present, be sure to scrub the catchment surface area with salt water and rinse it well. By doing this before it starts to rain, you will remove any heavy salt build up and residue that could foul the collected fresh rain water. (If water stores permit, it is better to rinse the catchment surface with fresh water or with a store of reusable "salt tainted" fresh water that has been set aside for just this purpose. This will help lessen the degree of salt contamination in the newly caught rain water supply.)
- If the catchment surface is a dry cloth, saturate the cloth in sea water and then wring it out. The amount of salt contamination will be negligible in comparison with the amount of rain water that would be lost in the cloth absorption.
- If you must improvise a catchment use any available material, preferably with low absorption qualities. Allow for a catchment pocket and then funnel the collected water into a container. Never mix newly collected water with your fresh water stores until you have had time to taste it and verify that it is not contaminated. Mixing newly collected water that is contaminated with salt into your fresh water stores will ruin your entire supply of water.

RATIONING

Rationing is determined by both the availability of supplies and the period that you wish to have the supplies last. Plan for a long period of isolation. This will motivate the crew to tighten rations and begin looking for a means to supplement the supplies.

DANGEROUS LIQUIDS

Acute stages of thirst can alter the victim's ability to reason. Survivors in desperate conditions have been known to swallow any form of liquid in their attempt to alleviate thirst. To the person in a healthy and hydrated state, the very notion of drinking dangerous liquids may seem incomprehensible. The possibility is nevertheless very real to the delirious castaway. The following "dangerous liquids" should be avoided at all costs:

- Battery water, because it contains sulfuric acid
- Kerosenes or lantern alcohol
- Alcohol, because it will not satisfy your body's need for water. It may also intoxicate you, which could induce vomiting and the loss of fluids. Alcohol absorbs water and accelerates the dehydration process.

SHORE WATER

Once on shore, it may be possible to obtain water by digging holes at about 100 yards above the high tide mark (at low tide). Filter the water through a "sand filter" to improve the taste. It may be brackish, but it is usually safe to drink. Test for salt content by tasting a small amount.

If there are sand dunes present, look in the hollows between them for visible water or moist sand, and dig for water there.

8

Edible and Hazardous Marine Life

NEARLY EVERY ORGANISM THAT LIVES IN OR around the sea is a potential food source. Emergency rations should not be used as a primary source of food, but should be used to supplement whatever food can be obtained from the environment.

TEST FOR EDIBILITY

Before consuming any type of fresh food that you are not absolutely certain is safe, always test for edibility with very small portions of the food. You will probably, at one time or another, experience some degree of food poisoning. But if you utilize the following test for every source of food, the chances of severe poisoning will be greatly minimized. This test does not apply to food that has been spoiled.

- Touch the food to the tip of the tongue. If it burns, stings, or tastes bad, throw it away and wash your hands immediately.
- If it tastes acceptable, leave a little in the mouth for five minutes. If you have no adverse reaction, then swallow it, and wait one hour.

- If there is still no reaction, eat a small serving and wait another hour.
- If you have not had any adverse reactions to the food after testing it, then it should be relatively safe to eat since most poisons (except those caused by spoilage) will produce symptoms within a very short time.
- If no adverse symptoms occur within 12 hours after eating a small portion of the food, it can be considered edible.
- Do not assume that all fish of the same species are edible (particularly those species in which ciguatera poisoning might be suspected). A test should be applied to each fish before consuming it.
- If there is any doubt about the edibility of a food source, throw it out. Don't take any chances.

PLANKTON AND SEAWEED
Seaweed

Many seaweeds are edible, and are a nutritional food source. Seaweed should be washed in fresh water before being eaten, and can be eaten raw or dried. (Some types of seaweed are poisonous, so an edibility test should always be applied.) The ingestion of seaweed requires gradual adaptation because of the laxative quality of its high cellulous content.

The leafy green seaweeds can be easily dried for storage, and are a good source of protein and carbohydrates. The value of encountering pieces of seaweed floating in the open sea is that tiny animals (small fish, crabs, and shrimp) can be found clinging to them. These fish are excellent sources of food or bait, and are easily dislodged by shaking the clumps of seaweed.

Plankton

Plankton includes minute plants and animals that drift about in the ocean. The nutritional values of plankton are high, but because of their high chiton and cellulose content they can not be digested in large quantities. There are also toxic species that can be hard to detect. It is therefore not advisable to consume plankton in the survival situation other than as a last resort, always applying an edibility test before consuming it.

- If it is necessary to use plankton as a food source, you must have a sufficient supply of fresh water for drinking.
- Plankton can be caught by dragging a fine woven net or cloth through the water. It can be eaten raw or cooked.
- The gelatinous plankton species should be discarded, since their tissues are composed primarily of salt water.
- Examine the catch and sort out any broken stinging jelly-fish tentacles that you might have inadvertently caught.
- Be cautious of consuming plankton in the areas and seasons where red tides are known to occur.

SHELLFISH POISONING

Red Tides

Red tides are caused by the proliferation or sudden "bloom" of minute species of plankton called *dinoflagellates*. These planktonic algae are toxic to man. The plankton "blooms" also cause paralytic shellfish poisoning, which can be fatal. It is transmitted to man by ingesting shellfish that have been feeding in red tide areas.

Red tides occur in waters above 30 degrees north latitude and below 30 degrees south latitude. Most outbreaks occur between May and October, when water temperatures are the highest. Survivors in tropical waters, or those in temperate waters during the winter months, need not be concerned about the occurance of red tides.

It is important to note that poisonous shellfish cannot be detected by their smell or appearance. Mussels, clams, oysters, and scallops are the main vehicles of transmission.

Because of the severity of the poisoning, preventive measures are extremely important.

Symptoms of Paralytic Shellfish Poisoning

* Tingling of the lips, mouth, face, and extremities frequently accompanied by nausea and diarrhea
* Muscle paralysis and respiratory impairment in more severe cases

Most symptoms usually appear within 30 minutes of ingesting a toxic mollusk. Most deaths occur within the first 12 hours of illness from respiratory paralysis.

Treatment

Induce vomiting to clear the gastrointestinal tract as soon as possible. Place victim lying down out of the sun. Artificial respiration might be required in severe cases.

FISH

Fish is a nutritious source of food, rich in protein as well as other minerals and elements. Ocean fish can be eaten raw. Fresh water fish should never be eaten raw, because they can introduce parasites into your digestive system. Cooking fresh water fish first is the only method of preventing this.

Spoilage

Fish spoils within hours without any means of refrigeration, particularly in warm tropical climates. Freshly caught fish should be placed out of direct sunlight and should be cleaned immediately. All fish that is not immediately cleaned and eaten or preserved may spoil within three to six hours. Do not eat fish that is suspected of being spoiled.

- Do not eat fish with an offensive odor (especially around the gills or belly), or that appear excessively slimy with a dull looking skin.
- Do not eat a fish if the flesh remains deeply indented when pressing in on it with the thumb, it is probably stale.
- If a fish has a sharp or peppery taste, it should be discarded. This is especially true of ocean fish with dark-colored flesh.
- Do not eat fish that have been left in the sun more than two hours without having been gutted and preserved.
- Cooking cannot be relied upon to make spoiled fish safe to eat.
- Do not eat the skin, head, or internal organs, especially the gonads and liver, of any fish you do not know for certain to be entirely edible. The liver, gonads, brain, and other organs can be poisonous in an otherwise edible species of fish. They should always be given the edibility test.

POISONOUS FISH

Poisonous fish are widely distributed throughout the world, but are most common in tropical and semitropical waters, particularly in the tropical Pacific and the West Indies. As a general rule, most poisonous fish are found in shallow waters around shoals, reefs, and inlets. Therefore, the safest fish to eat are those from the open sea or deeper water beyond reefs. In open ocean situations, spoilage, rather than poisoning, will usually be your main concern.

Fresh fish that are poisonous to eat fall into two categories: those that are inherently poisonous, and those that develop toxins when their diets include toxic materials, the most common being ciguatera toxins.

Inherently Poisonous Fish

Fish that are inherently poisonous are easy to recognize and should never be eaten. They include:

- Porcupine fish, which can puff up and are covered with spines
- Puffer fish, which can swell up and become balloon-like
- Sunfish (molas), which look like a large head with no tail or body section (Figs. 8-1 through 8-3)

As a rule, avoid eating any type of fish that has spines or bristles instead of scales.

Toxic Ciguatera Poisoning

Ciguatera poisoning is the most prevalent type of poisoning known. Almost any fish living in the sea can be a potential carrier of ciguatoxin, although it occurs mainly among inshore fish of tropical and subtropical islands. There is no way to detect a toxic fish by its appearance, and the toxin cannot be destroyed by any method of rinsing or cooking.

Fig. 8-1 Porcupine fish

Fig. 8-2 Puffer fish

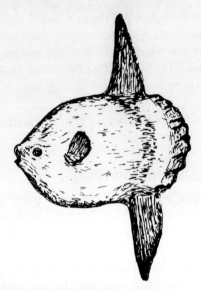

Fig. 8-3 Ocean Sunfish/Mola mola

Geographical distribution does not give adequate warning of toxicity. Toxicity can vary from one locality to another. The same species of fish on one reef that is edible can be found to be toxic in an adjacent reef. Ciguatera poisoning is thought to be caused by toxic coral vegetation that bottom fish feed on. Consequently, ciguatera builds into the whole food chain in a cumulative manner (Fig. 8-4).

Precautions. In a tropical area known to have ciguatoxic fish, take the following precautions when eating reef fish:

- Do not eat large predatory fish that may have fed on other toxic fish (barracuda, snapper, grouper, amberjack, and moray eels). These are most dangerous, because of their larger concentrations of accumulated toxins. A good rule of thumb is not to eat any fish over 30 inches in affected areas, since large fish have a higher concentration of toxins.

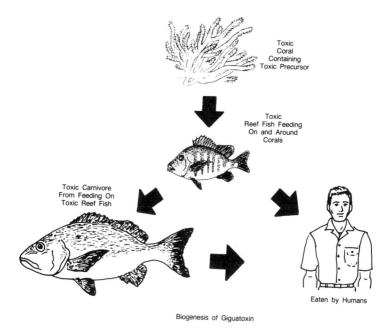

Toxic
Coral
Containing
Toxic Precursor

Toxic
Reef Fish Feeding
On and Around
Corals

Toxic Carnivore
From Feeding On
Toxic Reef Fish

Eaten by Humans

Biogenesis of Giguatoxin

Fig. 8-4 Ciguatoxin poisoning occurs through the food chain.

- Be extremely cautious of bottom dwelling shore fish near reefs. These are most likely to be toxic, and include such species as surgeonfish and parrotfish, as well as mullet, triggerfish, and porgies (especially fish with a parrot-like beak). More than 400 species have been reported as ciguatoxic at one time or another (Figs. 8-5 through 8-9).

- Never eat the liver, intestines, roe, and head of reef-dwelling fish, since these have the highest concentration of toxins. Be careful not to puncture the innards when cleaning fish, toxins can spread to the flesh.

- Always apply an edibility test before eating. Always eat small portions, since toxicity is directly related to the amount eaten.

- Eat fish only once or twice a week, since the toxin has a cumulative effect. Fish that are only mildly toxic in themselves can add up to give a severe intoxication over a consecutive period of consumption.

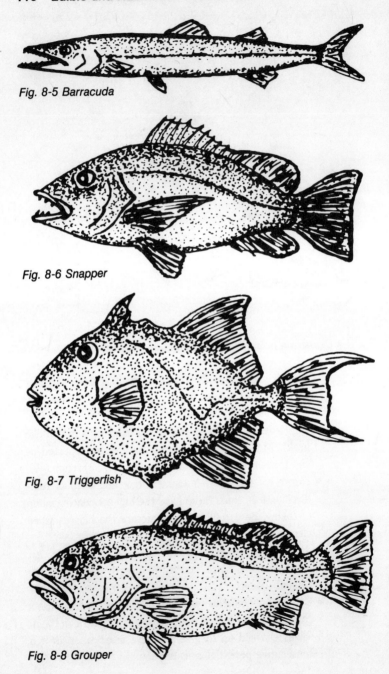

Fig. 8-5 Barracuda

Fig. 8-6 Snapper

Fig. 8-7 Triggerfish

Fig. 8-8 Grouper

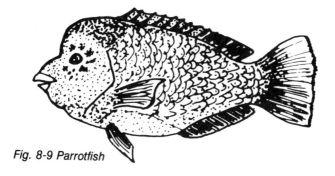

Fig. 8-9 Parrotfish

- Soaking the fish in several changes of seawater, or bringing it to a boil several times in different water may reduce some of the toxins, but this is not always reliable. It is only a precautionary measure at best.

Symptoms. Some common symptoms of nonbacterial fish poisoning include:

- Abdominal pain, vomiting, and diarrhea
- Tingling and numbness of the lips
- Dizziness and weakness

In severe cases, symptoms are pronounced and can lead to muscular paralysis and convulsions. Coma and death from respiratory paralysis can occur, although this is somewhat rare.

Ciguatera can develop in about 3 to 5 hours after the fish is eaten. All of the symptoms except for the feeling of weakness will generally subside within 24 hours.

Treatment. The stomach should be emptied immediately to get rid of any remaining poison. After that, alleviate the symptoms as best you can. Antihistamines may relieve the itching, and rest is recommended.

STINGING FISH

Survivors floating in the open ocean will have little cause to worry about the following species of stinging fish, since they are all reef dwelling and bottom dwelling creatures. If, however, you are stranded near a shoal area and foraging for food among the reefs, be extremely cautious of encountering fish with stinging spines and venomous glands.

Toxicity can vary between species and individual fish, but the following groups of fish are known to be hazardous: (Figs. 8-10 and 8-11)

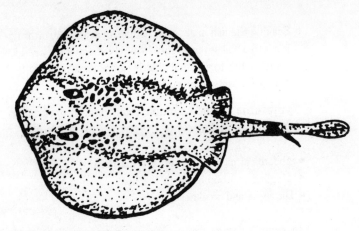

Fig. 8-10 Scorpionfish

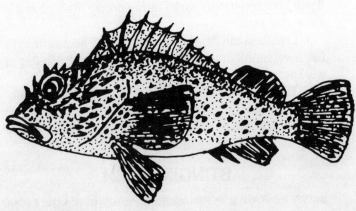

Fig. 8-11 Stingray

- Stingrays
- Catfish
- Weeverfish, toadfish, and stargazers
- Surgeonfish
- Stonefish, zebra fish, and scorpion fish

Observe the following precautions regarding species of fish with spines that can cause puncture wounds and that may contain venom:

- Wear foot protection when wading in shallow water. Most spiny fish will not move from your path.
- Slide your feet with a shuffling motion when wading along muddy or sandy bottoms to avoid stepping on sting rays or other sharp-spined fish.
- Do not stick your bare hand into ledges or holes. Always use a stick.
- Avoid handling fish with venomous spines even after the fish is dead, since the spines can remain toxic.

If the poison glands are removed, the flesh of some venomous species may be edible. The hazards involved in removing the spines and glands make them an impractical food source.

First Aid for Venomous Puncture Wounds

- Cleanse and flush the wound immediately.
- Place the wounded area in hot water (as hot as the victim can stand) or use hot compresses for 30 to 60 minutes to deactivate the toxins.
- Cut out sting ray barbs because the barb is shaped like an arrow point.

MORAY EELS

Tropical eels should never be consumed, because they are known carriers of ciguatoxins. Moray eels in temperate and cold-water climates, or in areas known to be unaffected by ciguatera poisons, are edible, and the light, chickenlike meat can be consumed after the skin has been removed.

The aggressive reputation of the moray eel is generally exaggerated as a marine hazard to man, but suffice it to say a moray eel has sharp, pointed teeth and will defend its territory when provoked. Morays live in holes and crevices, so never reach into an underwater hole without first checking it for eels. The bite is not toxic, but is easily infected and can be difficult to heal in humid, tropical areas (Fig. 8-12).

SHARKS

Of the more than 350 species of sharks, there are only about 24 that are considered dangerous to man. The presence of shark is commonly reported by castaways in survival platforms. However, they are often reported as more of a nuisance than an actual hazard, due to their tendency

Fig. 8-12 Moray eels, when provoked or surprised around shallow reefs can inflict puncture wounds. (Photo by Michael Farley)

to bump and bang against the underside of a life craft (Figs. 8-13 through 8-16).

The majority of shark attacks occur in tropical waters, but this may be simply because more people swim in warm waters than in cold waters. While it is not known what actually motivates shark attacks, a desire for food and defense of territory seem to suggest the strongest motivations.

Exercise preventive measures in shark-infested waters to eliminate the stimuli that attract sharks:

- Avoid erratic movements, which produce sound waves underwater.
- Stay out of water where fish, animal blood, or offal have been dumped, these odors may attract sharks. Only dump offal when you are underway.
- Avoid trailing any part of your body in the water, such as dangling arms or legs from a life raft.

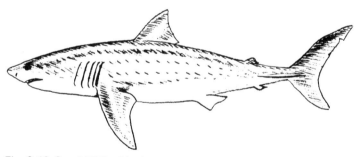

Fig. 8-13 Great White Shark

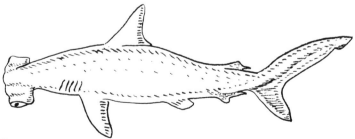

Fig. 8-14 Hammerhead Shark

Fig. 8-15 Blue Shark

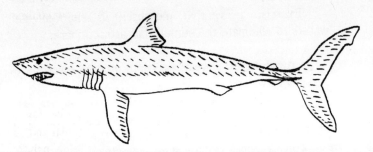

Fig. 8-16 Mako Shark

- Discourage a shark that threatens to attack or damage the life raft, jabbing at its snout or gills with an oar.

Shark Repellent

New shark defenses are continually being tested, but as yet, nothing has been found to be foolproof. The shark screen is one of the most promising deterrents. It is composed of an opaque plastic bag with several inflatable flotation collars that protect the enclosed swimmer by eliminating most of the sounds, smells, and visual stimuli that attract sharks. A black plastic bag, large enough to envelop a person, can also be improvised to do the same thing.

Food

Shark meat is a good food source. It can be eaten raw, dried, or cooked. Although most sharks are edible, the flesh of tropical and arctic sharks should only be eaten with caution. In many cases, the flesh might be mildly toxic, and can cause gastrointestinal upset and diarrhea. Shark meat spoils rapidly, because of the high urea content in the blood. The meat should be bled immediately or soaked in several changes of water.

The most severe forms of poisoning usually result from eating shark liver, which can cause nausea, diarrhea, muscular paralysis, and even death. It is a good idea to avoid eating any shark liver, unless you are absolutely sure that it is edible. Unlike most other fish, the spinal column of a shark contains no fluid.

OTHER MARINE HAZARDS

Jellyfish and Portuguese Man-of-War

These sea creatures can usually always be found floating on the surface of the water. Some jellyfish and all Portuguese man-of-war are capable of inflicting painful stings that may cause allergic reactions in some individuals. Sea Wasps are an extremely dangerous, though uncommon, jellyfish that inhabit the waters around Australia, the Phillipines, and the Indian Ocean. Their sting can be fatal; death can occur within seconds or minutes (Fig. 8-17).

Treatment. Several methods for treating jellyfish stings have been recommended by medical authorities:

- Remove the tentacles; gently pull the tentacles off the skin, or shave the area with a razor or knife. Never rub the tentacles with sand or a towel.
- Apply alkaline solutions to the area to help neutralize the toxin. Ammonia, urine, sodium bicarbonate, meat tenderizer, papaya juice, or any liquid with a high alcohol content can be used. Apply a hot water compress or immerse the area that was stung in hot water to deactivate the toxins.
- Apply an alkaline solution to the affected area prior to removing the tentacles, to prevent additional irritations during their removal. Then apply a drying paste (powder,

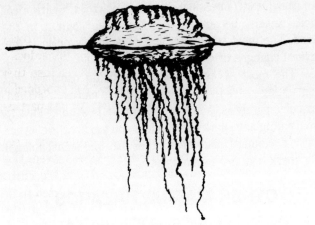

Fig. 8-17 Some types of open ocean jellyfish, such as the Portuguese man-of-war, can inflict serious stings on the unwary swimmer.

flour, or dry sand) to the skin, and scrape it off the skin along with the stinging cells.

- Treatment for shock or respiratory difficulties may be necessary if a severe reaction develops.

Sea Snakes

Sea snakes are highly poisonous, and are found only in the Pacific and Indian oceans. They vary widely in color patterns, but are snakelike in appearance and are best identified by their vertically flattened tail and scaled body. Their small mouth and nonaggressive nature usually makes them less dangerous than many land snakes, but their venom is about ten times deadlier than any other snake.

Sea snakes are edible, once the head containing the venom glands has been removed. Handle a sea snake with extreme caution. They are commonly eaten in many areas of Asia.

Sea Urchins

Sea urchins are abundant around reefs and rocky shore areas worldwide. Any sea urchin can be hazardous if accidentally stepped on or brushed against because they have slender and sharp spines, which become imbedded in skin. The danger of infection, in tropical areas, is a particular hazard with sea urchin wounds.

Treatment. If a puncture wound occurs from a sea urchin, extract those spines that are easily removed. Dissolve the rest by applying ammonia, alcohol, or citrus juice. Diesel fuel and urine have also been reported to be effective.

Food Source. Sea urchin roe is considered a delicacy, and may be eaten either raw or cooked. The roe sacs can be extracted by slicing through the sea urchin with a heavy, sharp knife and carefully removing the brightly colored (yellow or orange) clusters of eggs.

Cone Shells

Poisonous species of cone shells are most commonly found in the tropical Indian and Pacific Oceans. Those shells with a textured color pattern or a red proboscis are most likely to be toxic. The open end of the shell may contain a poisonous, hypodermic-like tooth, which can produce acute pain, swelling, paralysis, blindness, or even death, in less than three hours.

Cone shells are found under rocks, in crevices of coral reefs, and along rocky shores or protected bays. Avoid handling any shells that look like cones (Fig. 8-18).

Coral

Coral cuts are one of the most common hazards in tropical waters. The razor-sharp edges of coral can cause deep and severe cuts that are notorious for becoming infected, and slow to heal. Always wear shoes and clothing around coral reef areas to protect exposed parts of the body.

Fig. 8-18 When foraging around shallow reefs, be cautious handling cone-shaped shells.

Fire coral is not a true coral, but looks very much like a smooth coral. It will sting any bare skin that brushes against it, producing an irritating rash. The rash should be treated with antiseptics to minimize the chance of infection.

TURTLES

Turtles will often approach and bump the life raft, and represent a well-documented source of food for the survivor. If the turtle is too large to bring aboard or if the castaway is too weak to haul an uncooperative turtle aboard, you can secure the animal to the raft and weaken it or drown it first. The claws and beak of a turtle are very sharp and can cause injuries to the raft or the castaway. To prevent this, always bring the turtle aboard cautiously, while holding the hind flippers (Fig. 8-19). Once a turtle has been brought on board, cut its throat on the underside and sever the neck arteries. This preserves the quality of the meat for storage by allowing the animal to bleed to death. This method will also yield a sizable amount of fresh blood, which can be "caught" and drank immediately, before it cools and begins to coagulate. (Note: If the animal

Fig. 8-19 Sea turtles are a welcome source of food for the survivor.

is not immediately bled upon death, the meat might not keep well.)

- Eat the eggs, heart, and meat, but discard the offal or use it for bait. The shell can also be put to useful purposes.
- Avoid eating too much turtle liver. Excessive concentrated liver oil can cause illness.
- Collect any fat and oil from turtles. They can be used for lubricating or protection purposes.
- Break the bones and extract the marrow for nourishment.

BIRDS

Although marine birds are difficult to catch, they provide a good addition to the diet.

- All birds can be eaten.
- Skin them, rather than pluck them.
- Bone marrow provides good nourishment and can be

eaten by breaking or chewing the bone and extracting the marrow.

- Utilize all parts of the bird, including the feathers, which can be used for insulation in your clothing or even as fish hooks.

To trap a bird:

- Float bait on a small piece of wood to try to attract a bird.
- Toss the bait into the air to attract a bird.
- Don't attempt to grab a bird until it has folded its wings.
- Use a slingshot.

DRYING MEAT

The method of "sun-drying" meat or fish for storage purposes is often the only available way. Fresh-caught fish that is well dried can be edible for days. (*Note:* It is not advisable to store fish by treating the flesh with salt in the survival situation. The last thing you want to do is to ingest salt when water supplies are limited.)

The procedure for sun drying is simple:

- Clean the catch and discard the offal (or use for bait).
- Cut the meat into thin strips about 1 inch in thickness.
- Allow the strips to hang in the air and sun. This will dry the meat out without losing the nourishment in it. The meat can be eaten at any stage of its drying process.
- Consume the meat when ample water is available. Since the dried meat is dehydrated, body fluids will be needed to digest and assimilate it.

VITAMIN DEFICIENCIES

A person whose diet is lacking in certain vitamins for a prolonged period of time will suffer vitamin deficiencies. As the deprivation is prolonged, certain physical symptoms will begin to surface. The following list indicates vitamin deficiency according to its symptoms, as well as what types of food you might find in the survival situation to help remedy this condition:

- Vitamin A deficiency will cause night blindness and muscular weakness. Actual blindness in the acute stages may occur. Vitamin A can be found in the following:
  egg yolk
  fat
  liver
  fish oils
- Vitamin B (thiamine) deficiency will cause fatigue, headache, and eventually beriberi. Vitamin B can be found in the following:
  egg yolk
  lean meat

- Vitamin B2 (riboflavin) deficiency will cause irritations of the digestive tract. Vitamin B2 can be found in a variety of foods such as:
  lean meat
  eggs
  liver
- Vitamin C deficiency will cause loss of teeth, nosebleeds, hemmorages under the skin, and eventually scurvy. Vitamin C can be found in the following:
  fruits
  liver
  fish eyes, brains, and pancreas (small amounts)
- Vitamin D deficiency will eventually manifest itself in disease affecting bone condition, known as rickets. Vitamin D can be found in:
  liver oils
  fish oils

9

Survival in Cold Climates

BASIC SKILLS AND PROCEDURES ARE SIMILAR in most survival locations. In colder regions, however, where extremely low air and water temperatures prevail, specialized skills and equipment are necessary.

The ability to stay warm in areas of extreme cold is of paramount importance. The capability to regulate and conserve your body heat may mean the difference between life and death. This is not based as much on skill and ingenuity as it is on having the proper equipment and the knowledge of how to use it.

HEAT REGULATION

The regulation of body heat loss is a primary concern in cold climates. The type of clothing you wear is one of the most important factors influencing heat loss.

You must wear proper clothing that will trap a narrow layer of air next to the skin. This zone of air is warmed by the heat generated from the body, and your clothes serve as an insulator to retain this warm air.

Materials such as animal fur, down, and wool are made up of thousands of tiny air pockets. They efficiently produce a "dead air" zone next to the skin. Several layers of clothing are usually more effective in retaining and controlling heat than a single, bulky garment.

Exposure to wind and wetness will affect the efficiency of the warm-air zone under your clothes. Wet clothing and cold wind will transfer the heat out of this zone faster than the body's heat generating system can replace it. This exposes you to the dangers of hypothermia. If clothing becomes sopping wet it should be removed, wrung out and only worn again if no dry clothes are available.

COLD CLIMATE CRUISING

When cruising in cold climates have a survival suit for each crew member. These suits are made of highly efficient insulating materials and will enable you to withstand cold temperatures far better than regular clothing. There are many types of survival suits available to the consumer, from well-insulated flotation jackets to actual dry suits that provide complete protection by totally sealing out the water (Figs. 9-1 and 9-2).

A neoprene vest or wetsuit in your provisions can serve as a practical piece of gear. They provide insulation and protection from the elements and are efficient as an alternative in an emergency situation. It should be noted, however, that wearing a wetsuit can cause unwanted perspiration and may not be advisable.

Figure 9-3 shows a U-Vic Thermofloat jacket. This design has protective qualities for guarding against hypothermia.

DEHYDRATION

The possibility of losing too much body fluid and causing a state of dehydration can be a serious problem in cold climates. If the water ration is low, dehydration can begin

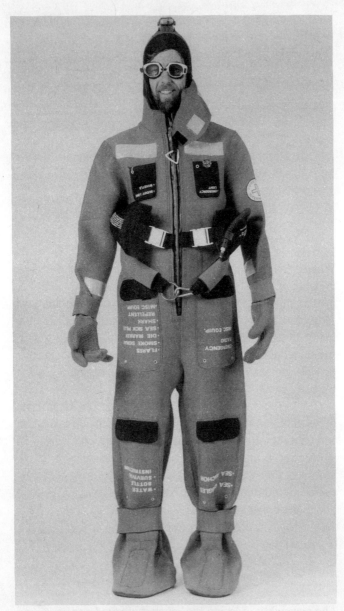

Fig. 9-1 Being properly equipped with a survival suit can greatly extend survival time in cold waters. (Photo courtesy Survival International Inc.)

Fig. 9-2 Survival Suit. (Photo courtesy STEARNS)

Fig. 9-3 U-VIC Thermo Floatation Jacket. (Photo courtesy Mustang)

its harmful effects on the body, and only the intake of water can remedy it. Furthermore, during strenuous labor in cold climates the body may perspire a lot, but the victim will not feel the natural thirst for water as he would in hot climates. Consequently, he may not feel inclined to replace the lost body fluids, and this can seriously contribute to dehydration.

EXPOSURE

There are a number of physiological complications that can arise as a result of exposure to severe cold. The unique characteristic of survival in severe cold climates is that the initial actions you undertake must be the correct ones and must be taken immediately. This is extremely important because cold and freezing temperatures can adversely affect the body rapidly. The foremost danger, of course, is that of freezing to death.

Review and understand the following maladies and physiological processes to know how to minimize their dangers in cold climates:

Hypothermia

Hypothermia occurs when the temperatures within the central body core reach a subnormal level. When the core temperature drops below 90°F (approx. 32°C) serious complications begin to develop and death may occur when the core temperature drops to 80°F (30°C).

In the unfortunate event of cold water immersion, remember some additional points concerning hypothermia:

- If you are wearing a flotation device, less body heat will be lost by remaining still in the water rather than swimming or treading water. Curling up into a fetal position can increase your survival time.
- About 50% of your body heat is lost from the head area. When immersed try to keep your head as far out of the water as possible.
- If there are several people in the water, huddling close together can help preserve body heat.

- Even if a person appears dead from hypothermia or cold water drowning, continue artificial ventilation and circulation as long as possible. When a person falls into water with a temperature of 70°F or less, an involuntary response called the mammalian diving reflex might be triggered. This reflex automatically shuts down the flow of oxygen to all but the most vital areas—the heart, lungs, and brain—sustaining life for remarkable periods of time without breathing. In one case a college student survived without ill effects after being submerged for 38 minutes.

Frostbite

Frostbite is an ever present danger in freezing temperatures. It affects the extremities of the body first. Its onset and symptoms are often difficult to detect. Familiarize yourself with both the symptoms and prevention of frostbite, which are covered in depth in Chapter 10.

Immersion Foot

Immersion foot occurs as a result of prolonged exposure of the lower extremities to waters just above freezing temperatures. Since it is difficult to keep water out of the life raft, immersion foot is a constant threat in cold water climates. The symptoms and prevention of immersion foot are covered in Chapter 10.

Snow Blindness

Snow blindness is caused by brilliant reflections and glare off of snow and ice. It can occur even on cloudy days and is very painful and debilitating. Symptoms include:

- A loss in the ability to detect the horizon (differentiating between land's horizon and the sky)
- A burning sensation in the eyes
- Pain, which can be felt when the eyes are exposed to even the weakest light

Prevention is the best medicine; but complete darkness is the best available cure once a person is stricken with snow blindness. Prevention can consist of wearing sunglasses or some other type of eye shade. You can improvise with wood or leather by making a narrow slit for each eye and wearing them as you would sunglasses (Fig. 9-4). This reduces the amount of glare entering the eye. Black soot applied to the nose and cheeks will also help to reduce glare.

Sunburn

It is possible to get a severe sunburn even on cloudy days. It is best to prevent sunburn before the need for treatment arises. If possible, leave no part of the body exposed. Be attentive to those who are asleep or ill, and make sure their bodies are protected from the sun. Sunburn can come on gradually and may go unnoticed until it is too late.

Fig. 9-4 Eye shades can be improvised to protect the vision from sun glare.

Carbon Monoxide (CO) Poisoning

In close, closed quarters where fire is used to produce warmth, carbon monoxide poisoning can be a danger. Any use of fire, even with heaters or lamps, can produce a dangerous amount of odorless carbon monoxide fumes that can be fatal. Proper ventilation will prevent this type of poisoning.

Icebergs

Icebergs are constantly melting and repositioning themselves. The melting process is faster below the water line than it is above the water line. Consequently, icebergs become top heavy and topple over, creating peril for anything and anyone nearby. Avoid icebergs that are pinnacled. For shelter, seek out low, flat ice-bergs.

FOOD

Fish

Almost all freshly caught sea fish are edible and nutritious when eaten raw. Since cold climates act as refrigeration, fish are less susceptible to spoilage than in warmer climates. A fish can be effectively preserved by slicing it into thin strips and hanging it to dry.

Mammals

Most large arctic mammals, such as seals and walruses, are difficult to approach and will generally avoid man. Because of their large size, most are capable of inflicting injuries and should be approached cautiously. Almost all marine mammals are a viable food source if they can be caught. The liver, especially in arctic and cold-water mammals, should not be eaten because of their frequent toxic concentrations of Vitamin A.

Birds

Sea birds can be used for food. Fresh eggs are edible at any stage of embryo development.

WATER

- Always melt snow before consuming it. The body heat required to melt snow in the body after it has been consumed may be too valuable to waste. Snow may be melted by holding it in your hands, if conditions permit. (Watch for the onset of frostbite.)

- Melt ice rather than snow. Ice will yield more water per volume, and it requires less heat and time to melt.

- Sea ice loses its salt content after approximately one year, then it becomes an excellent source of water. "Old" sea ice can be distinguished by its bluish color and rounded corners. Newer ice that still contains salt will appear grayish, milky, and hard. Do not drink it.

- The salt can be removed from sea water in freezing climates by the following method: Collect seawater in a container and allow it to freeze. Fresh water freezes first and thus the salt will concentrate as a slush in the center or core of the container. Remove this core of salt, remelt the ice, and it will be sufficiently salt free to keep you alive.

ICING AT SEA

Icing at sea can present a serious hazard to smaller ships and vessels. The added weight of ice reduces the range of a vessel's stability, particularly when icing occurs on the masts, rigging, and superstructure. Vessels may become top heavy and capsize. The accumulation of ice on aerials can render radar or radios inoperative.

Freezing Rain

Freezing rain can cover a ship with a fresh-water glaze of ice. This accumulated weight of ice is unlikely to directly endanger a ship.

Arctic Frost Smoke

Arctic frost smoke or white frost occurs in temperatures below 32°F. Small water droplets in the frost smoke are supercooled. Part of the droplet freezes immediately when contact is made with a craft. The result is an accumulation of white "rime" ice. (It is easier to remove rime ice than clear ice or glaze because it is porous.)

Freezing Spray

The most dangerous form of icing is freezing spray. It occurs when the air temperature is below the freezing temperature of sea water (27°F). Spray freezes on exposed surfaces to produce clear ice or glaze. The lower the air temperature and the stronger the wind, the more rapidly ice will accumulate.

It must be understood that as ice forms on areas that are exposed to spray (such as the rails and rigging), the affected surface area increases in size allowing for an even greater and rapid accumulation of ice.

SURVIVAL TIPS

Breathing. In severe cold temperatures, breathe only through your nose. This helps to warm the air before it reaches your lungs and will lessen the danger of frosting them.

Navigation. In polar regions, a magnetic compass may not be as reliable as in other areas. The compass may react sluggishly and inconsistently. It is advisable to take the average of several readings in order to increase accuracy.

Blood. Blood is affected by cold temperatures. It may take longer to clot and will appear to be thinner.

Urine. Urine can be a source of heat, if necessary. If, for instance, your body touches a frozen metal object, it may freeze onto it. Forcibly removing it may cause tearing of the skin. Urine can act to thaw the part so that it can be safely removed.

Exposure. Be careful not to expose more of your body than is necessary (such as for bowel movements).

Body Heat. Huddling together can help contain and share body heat, but take care not to promote hypothermia in your own body by warming a wet or frostbitten victim.

Landfall. In the arctic regions, snow-covered land areas or large ice fields are often indicated by light colored reflections on clouds. This is markedly different from the normal darkish gray reflection caused by open ocean.

10

Survival Medicine

THIS CHAPTER CONTAINS MEDICAL INFORMA-
tion with the specific needs of the castaway in mind. It
focuses primarily on the survival situation in which a minimal amount of medicines and equipment (if any) is available, and it addresses those emergencies and problems
that are most likely to occur. The emphasis is on a lay-
man's diagnosis and improvisation of treatment, rather
than the application of medicines and dosages normally
prescribed or recommended by a physician. How effective
you are concerning medical treatment and the usage of
drugs is your decision entirely, since a comprehensive
coverage of either subject does not fall within the scope of
this book. This is not a complete medical summary, nor is
it meant to be a substitution for a professional medical
book. Rather, it is designed to effectively illustrate the
symptoms and treatment of a variety of physical maladies
to which the castaway is most commonly exposed.

SURVIVAL FIRST AID

In the survival situation, the definition of first aid must be
expanded to include final aid. Since professional medical

treatment is not normally available in an emergency situation, all injuries must be dealt with in a complete and final manner.

Minor Injuries

First aid treatment for minor injuries is designed to "contain and treat" the injury in order to minimize the possibility of complications and to promote speedy recovery.

Major Injuries

First aid when applied to major or massive injuries is the attempt to neutralize and stabilize the injury until proper medical treatment can be found.

In the survival situation the understanding and early recognition of medical problems is crucial for two primary reasons:

- The lack of adequate drugs, medical services, and equipment.
- The fact that many maladies can be avoided altogether or at least greatly minimized by early detection and treatment. Dehydration, hypothermia, and shock, for example, are grave threats to the exposed or injured castaway and early recognition of each of these is vital to their treatment.

HEAT EXHAUSTION

Heat exhaustion (also called heat prostration) is caused by a loss of water and salt from the body. Heat exhaustion results from exposure to high temperatures, and not necessarily just from exposure to direct sunlight. Cases of heat exhaustion are common among persons working in hot environments, such as engine rooms or furnace rooms, as well as outdoors in hot or humid conditions.

Heat exhaustion differs considerably from heatstroke, even though both conditions represent a failure in the body's mechanisms of regulating heat. While heat exhaustion can lead to collapse, it is much less serious than heatstroke.

Symptoms

- Skin appears pale and clammy
- Profuse sweating
- Weakness, dizziness, nausea, fainting
- Pulse will be fast and weak
- Breathing will be rapid and shallow
- Pupils dilated
- Mild muscular cramps (heat cramps)
- Body temperature below normal
- Possible headache and chills
- Dim or blurred vision

Treatment

To normalize the circulation of blood, effective treatment must restore salt and fluid to the body.

- Place the patient in the shade, away from the heat source if possible.
- Lay the patient in a reclining position with his head slightly lower than his feet. This will increase the flow of blood to the head.
- Keep the victim warm by covering him with blankets or clothing.
- Keep the victim rested and quiet, and protect him from excessive heat and physical activity until he has recovered.
- To treat heat cramps, remove the victim from the heat source and massage the affected areas to help relieve the cramps.

HEATSTROKE

Heatstroke is a much more dangerous condition than heat exhaustion, and should be considered a medical emergency.

Heatstroke occurs when the body's cooling system no longer functions, because of exposure to extremely high air temperatures or the combination of excessive humidity and moderately high temperatures. When the temperature of the blood rises, the body's primary source of heat loss (the evaporation of sweat) ceases to function. The body's temperature gradually increases, and if not stopped, will eventually lead to circulatory collapse and deep shock, or death.

It is vital to be able to recognize the early stages of heatstroke so that corrective measures can be taken while the process is still reversible.

Symptoms

- Sudden onset, with possible fainting, dizziness, convulsions or delirium.
- Skin is hot, flushed and dry, typically red in color. Absence of sweat.
- High body temperature; high blood pressure and generalized weakness.
- Strong and rapid pulse.
- Possible muscular twitching and visual disturbances.
- Headache, nausea, and vomiting.

Treatment

The onset of heatstroke requires immediate treatment to reduce the body temperatures in order to prevent possible brain damage or death. The most effective treatment is a liquid cooling bath. The victim should be placed in a bath of cool water.

A cooling bath can be a dunk in the ocean. (If shark is present, then saturate the victim and his clothing with cool sea water to bring his temperature down.)

If a cooling bath is not possible, move the victim to a cool or shaded area, have him lie down and loosen any constricting clothing.

Cover the skin with wet, cold towels, cloths, or blankets, changing them frequently as they get warm; or sponge the victim with cold water. Continue to cool down the victim until his temperature drops.

The body temperature should be taken every ten minutes if possible. The cooling process must be continued until the body temperature falls below 101°F (38.3°C). If a thermometer is not available, feel the skin from time to time, and watch for signs of improvement such as: lower temperature, presence of perspiration, normal facial color, and slower pulse and respirations.

It is important to massage the skin vigorously during the cooling procedure. This will prevent the constriction of blood vessels and will stimulate and accelerate the return of "cooled" surface blood to the overheated core of the body.

IMMERSION FOOT/TRENCH FOOT

Immersion foot and trench foot are both local cold injuries resulting from prolonged exposure of the lower extremities to waters just above freezing temperatures. Contributing factors include inactivity of the extremities, and restriction and immobilization of the limbs. Blood circulation is reduced, causing the feet and toes to become stiff, numb, discolored, and swollen. In acute stages, flesh may die and amputation of the foot or leg might become necessary.

It is important to diagnose this type of cold injury early, because the beginning stages cause numbness rather than pain, and can gradually and almost unnoticeably lead to acute stages.

Treatment

Treatment is limited. Terminate the exposure to the cold water as quickly as possible. Attempt to keep the feet dry and warm. Keep the legs in a horizontal position to increase the circulation.

FROSTBITE

Frostbite is the most serious of local injuries that can result from exposure. Frostbite is the freezing of a body part in which tissue destruction occurs. Superficial frostbite (sometimes referred to as *frost nip*) occurs when only the surface of the skin becomes frozen. In this instance, the surface will feel hard, but the underlying tissue will be soft and "spongy" when depressed. This type of frostbite can be treated by rewarming the area and ending exposure.

Typically, frostbite begins on the small areas of the extremities (nose, fingers, ears), but is capable of spreading into larger areas. If the freezing process continues and develops into "deep" unthawed frostbite, the areas will become completely hard and cannot be depressed. At this stage, the thawing process must be started quickly. Only time will enable you to determine the serious degree of frostbite that has occurred.

Symptoms

Frostbite is not very painful in the early stages. The patient will typically feel a numb, tingling sensation. It is important to recognize the onset of frostbite to prevent it from causing serious problems.

The effects of serious frostbite can be seen before they are felt. In cases of prolonged exposure:

- Ice crystals in the skin tissue cause the area to appear white or grayish-yellow in color.
- In 12 to 36 hours, blisters will appear on the surface and underlying tissues. The area will appear very swollen and red when it thaws, and gangrene and necrosis (loss of tissue) will follow.

Treatment

Immediate rewarming is the best treatment. Treat it as soon as possible, but introduce heat very gradually, to prevent the onset of shock.

There are two types of rapid rewarming techniques:

- The wet technique is the quickest and therefore the most ideal. After terminating exposure, place the victim in a bath of heated water (104° to 107°F or 40° to 42°C in temperature). This will most efficiently accomplish the warming process. If you do not have a thermometer, test the water with your finger or elbow to make sure it is not too hot.

- The dry warming technique is the use of blankets, the sharing of body heat or heat sources. This technique will take 3 to 4 times longer than wet warming.

There are certain things that should never be done when treating frostbite:

- Never try to forcibly remove frozen clothing (shoes, mittens, etc.). Place the frozen piece of clothing in lukewarm water until it becomes soft, and then gently remove it.

- Never attempt to thaw a frozen body area by exercising it.

- Never let the victim stand on frozen feet. This will only complicate problems by damaging tissue and breaking the skin.

- Never massage or rub frozen body areas. This may cause further tissue damage.

- Never soak frozen limbs in kerosene or oil.

- Never expose frozen body parts directly to an open flame or fire.

- Never use water over 111°F (44°C) to rewarm a patient or body part.

- Never thaw a frostbitten body area until you are sure that it will not be frostbitten again. The refreezing of a body part can result in irreparable damage.

GANGRENE AND AMPUTATION

Gangrene, briefly defined, is the localized death of soft tissues caused by loss of blood supply. It may follow an injury such as severe frostbite, where the freezing of tissues has cut off blood supply for prolonged periods. Gangrene may also develop when tourniquet pressure has been used to seal off the blood flow of an infected or bleeding limb for such an extended period of time that the tissues have died from lack of blood supply.

Gangrene provides an ideal condition for bacterial growth and the spread of infection to the "living" parts of the body. It is extremely dangerous and if allowed to go untreated, can be fatal.

Gangrene can be either dry or wet in appearance, is painful, and produces offensive-smelling liquid. If an injury becomes dark and hard, gangrene must be suspected. Advance stages of gangrene can be remedied only by amputation. (Note: The conditions, procedures, and ramifications of amputation are lengthy and complicated and are beyond the scope of this book.)

BLEEDING

The human body contains approximately 6 quarts of blood. The loss of anymore than one pint is considered both dangerous and life threatening. Hemorrhaging is when there is excessive bleeding and loss of blood.

Hemorrhaging of a major blood vessel (arm, neck, or thigh) can cause death in a matter of minutes. It is, therefore, vital to immediately stop or control any severe bleeding in a wounded person.

Only the restoration of breathing takes priority over the control of hemmorraging in an emergency.

External bleeding can be from arteries, veins, capillaries, or a combination of all three, and should be treated first by direct pressure to the wound. If profuse bleeding continues, a tourniquet must be applied. (See section on Tourniquets later in this chapter).

Internal bleeding occurs when vessels are ruptured and blood leaks into body tissue. This sometimes results from blows to the body or diseases (such as bleeding ulcers).

Remember: A little blood goes a long way! Things usually look worse than they are.

Control of Bleeding

The methods to control bleeding include:

Direct Pressure. The simplest method is to apply direct pressure with the hand to the wounded area. Use a sterile pad or clean cloth. Pressure will promote the formation of blood clots, compress shut the open blood vessels, and prevent germs from contaminating the open wound.

Elevation. If bleeding persists, try elevating the wounded area to utilize the force of gravity. This will also lower blood pressure.

Pressure Points. Apply pressure to the artery that supplies the blood to the wounded area. This technique should be used only if direct pressure and elevation of the limb are not successful (Fig. 10-1).

Tourniquet. Use a tourniquet as a last-resort measure only if all other methods fail.

Tourniquet

A tourniquet is a constricting band used to stop arterial bleeding (spurting vessels) of an extremity. It is a last-resort measure and should only be used when all other techniques have failed to control the excessive flow of blood.

The danger involved in applying a tourniquet is that all blood flow beyond the point of application is blocked. This can be extremely dangerous. By cutting off circulation for a prolonged period of time, tissue destruction can occur from lack of blood and oxygen. If tissue dies, removal by amputation might be necessary.

Caution should be exercised when applying a tourniquet. If applied too loosely, it will not stop the bleeding; if applied too tightly, it can severely damage muscle, nerves, and tissue. Remember, the purpose is to stop the bleeding.

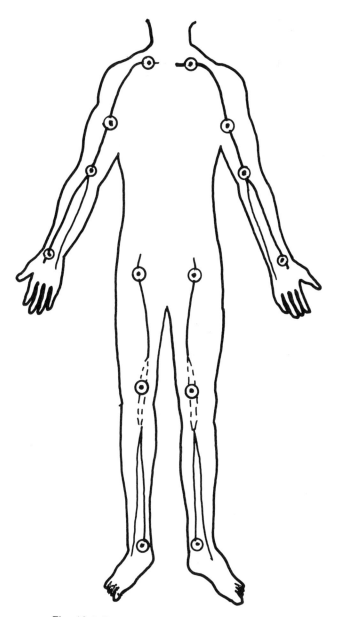

Fig. 10-1 Pressure points in the human body.

Improvising a tourniquet can be accomplished by using materials such as cloth, towels, tubing, belts, or anything that will provide a band around the limb. The band should ideally be at least 1 to 2 inches wide and long enough to encircle the limb twice (Fig. 10-2).

Applying a Tourniquet

- Place the tourniquet between the body trunk and the wound, (between the heart and the wound) approximately 2 to 4 inches above the injury. In the case of

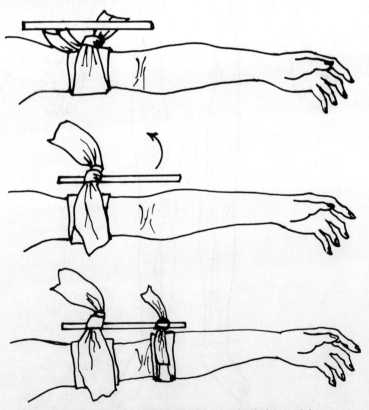

Fig. 10-2 The illustrations indicate proper methods for applying a tourniquet.

injuries just below the knee or elbow, it is advisable to apply the tourniquet above the knee or elbow. Never apply a tourniquet directly over a wound or fracture.

- Wrap the tourniquet material loosely around the limb and tie a simple knot (square knot).
- Lay a piece of wood or similar item over the tourniquet band and secure it with a single knot.
- Twist the stick several turns until the bleeding stops, but not tighter. While a tourniquet will stop the major spurting (hemorrhaging) of blood, some time may be required for the smaller veins to drain. Don't feel compelled to stop the minor bleeding. You may be tightening the tourniquet too much.
- Attach or fix the stick to the limb to maintain pressure. Secure the stick in place using another bandage, tape, or piece of cloth. (At this point, treat for shock and attend to the wound.)

Once the tourniquet has been properly applied, there are several points to keep in mind:

- Keep the treatment area as warm as possible.
- Never cover a tourniquet. The application of a tourniquet has been forgotten on occasion; and if the patient is unconscious or heavily sedated, he may not be aware of the treatment. (A forgotten tourniquet can be tragic.)
- Attach a note on the patient's clothing or elsewhere in an area that is clearly visible. Describe the location of the tourniquet and the date and time of its application.

Do not loosen or remove the tourniquet that was applied to stop the bleeding in the case of an amputated limb. It should be removed only under the advice and supervision of a physician.

Remember, permanent uninterrupted application of a tourniquet will result in death of the limb. Periodic loosening of the tourniquet will allow blood to flow into the limb long enough to keep the limb and tissues alive. The dangers of loosening a tourniquet (periodically or otherwise) are serious. Additional loss of blood occurs, which could promote shock and other complications. If the tissue is dead and infection or gangrene has set in, the loosening of the tourniquet will allow dangerous bacteria to flow into the "healthy" body.

A complete medical book should always be included in a yachtsman's library.

SPRAINS

Sprains are a common injury, especially in the wrist and ankle areas, caused by the extreme twisting or pulling of a joint and ligaments. Sprains can be quite painful and easily confused with a bone fracture.

Symptoms of Sprains

- Swelling
- Bruising
- Pain

Treatment

Apply cold wet packs, when available, to help relieve the pain and swelling. If possible, elevate the injured part. A splint can be applied if the sprain is severe.

FRACTURES

A fracture is a cracked or broken bone, usually occurring in the limbs of the body. There are two types of fractures: compound and simple.

Compound Fractures

A compound (open) fracture is considered a serious injury since the broken bone has pierced the skin and is protruding from the limb. There is constant danger of infection and contamination.

Treatment

- Scrub with soap and boiled (but cooled) water.
- Remove any foreign matter that is easily removable.
- Do not attempt to force the bone end back into place.
- Apply a sterile dressing and immobilize the fracture with a splint.
- Use antibiotics to prevent infection, and offer pain relievers if available.

Simple Fractures

A simple (closed) fracture is diagnosed when apparent symptoms indicate a broken bone. There is no open wound to speak of, but certain appearances in the limb, indicate a break: shortening or lengthening in the limb, deformity, crookedness, or perhaps the sound of a bone snapping. Sometimes only intense pain, swelling, or discoloration will be evident.

Treatment

- Do not move the fractured limb. Any improper movement can cause damage to tissue, nerves, and blood vessels.
- Apply a splint, if there is no obvious gross deformity, to immobilize the fracture. Padded splints are best, a pillow or bulky blanket will work.
- Apply a firm and steady pull in the direction of the normal axis of the bone, if very deformed, until alignment looks fairly normal. Do this as soon as possible after the injury. The pain will be greater if you wait to do it.
- Make sure that sensation (to pin prick) and circulation (pink fingers and toes) are present.
- Apply a firm compressive dressing if there is a large amount of swelling with elastic bandages and elevate the extremity for at least 2 hours.

Splints

* If a splint has not been included in your first aid kit, one can be improvised by simply fashioning a device that will keep the limb immobile. Boards, sticks, fishing poles, even magazines or dry newspaper, when folded properly, can work.

If no materials are available to improvise a splint, the limb can sometimes be secured to another limb, such as in the case of tying together two legs, fingers, or toes. Apply the splint snugly to prevent any slipping or further injury, but not so tightly that it prevents blood circulation in the limb (Fig. 10-3).

The splint should extend beyond both the joints above and below the injured limb. In the situation of a boat or raft on the ocean, it may be necessary to secure the injured limb, once the splint is applied, to the torso. This will help prevent movement of the limb caused by the raft's motion.

Recently a new type of splint has come into use. Made of a lightweight, transparent plastic that can be inflated by mouth like a balloon, in a matter of seconds. It can be stored in a small space.

DISLOCATIONS

Dislocations are usually obvious. Fingers and toes can be easily popped back into place with firm traction. After repositioning, splint the area in the normal resting position (natural curve) for at least 1 to 2 weeks. An injured toe can be splinted by taping it to an adjacent good toe with cotton between the toes.

For a dislocated shoulder, take pain medicine. Lie prone with the injured arm hanging over the edge of a platform far enough above the floor to allow you to hold a suspended bucket. Slowly fill the bucket with water as tolerated. This traction will eventually cause the shoulder to go back into place with a definite snap and pain relief.

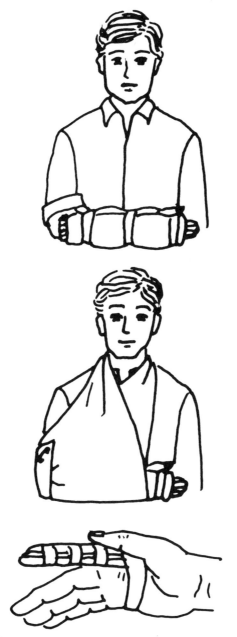

Fig. 10-3 Splints for fractured or broken bones.

INFECTIONS

Symptoms

- Red, painful, skin, often with red streaks.

Treatment

- Scrub with soap and water 2 to 4 times daily.
- Apply warm wet compresses.
- Elevate if the infection is on an extremity.

Urinary Tract Infection

Symptoms include burning on urination, blood in urine, urge to urinate frequently, or pain over kidney area, and fever. Take lots of fluids to keep the kidneys flushed, and appropriate medicine if available.

BURNS

Treatment

- First degree burns (red skin only): Cold soaks for 15 to 20 minutes. No other treatment is usually necessary.
- Second and third degree (skin blistered or sometimes white or charred): Cover area with mild soap (Phisohex) and wash gently. Follow this with a sterile nonadherent dressing. Change dressing periodically. If fever develops, take antibiotics.

WOUNDS

Wounds are generally broken down into five basic types:

Abrasion. An abrasion is an open wound caused by scraping the skin. It can be painful if the abraded area is very large. Bleeding from damaged capillaries and small veins is usually minimal.

Contusion. A contusion is a closed, superficial

wound usually the result of a blow from a blunt object. If the injury is located over a bone, there is a possibility of a fracture.

Puncture. A puncture is an open wound, usually with a small opening, and very dangerous if the object has penetrated deeply. An ice pick, for instance, would leave a small hole but could severely injure organs or cause internal hemorrhaging. External bleeding generally helps to cleanse a wound, but in the case of a puncture wound where less bleeding occurs, this cleansing process is minimal. Therefore, the possibility of infection is greater. Possible complications include lockjaw, tetanus, or gangrene.

Incision. An incision is usually caused by a sharp object. If the wound is deep, severe damage to muscles and nerves might occur. The amount of bleeding will depend on the depth of the cut.

Laceration. A laceration is caused by a ripping action (broken glass or moving machinery). This type of wound is jagged and irregular in appearance and may bleed more freely than an incised wound.

Diagnosing Wounds

Wounds vary as to the degree of damage sustained, and are designated: superficial, minor, major, massive, and complicated. The severity of a wound cannot always be determined at first glance. A wound from a nail for example, may appear minor, but if an internal organ were punctured, it could endanger your life; conversely the mangled surface skin on a scraped knee, though relatively minor, could appear more severe than it is.

It is important to acquaint yourself with first aid procedures for both minor and major wounds in order to quickly diagnose the extent of a wound and initiate proper treatment.

The possibility of infection is present in all types of wounds, no matter how minor, and should be treated accordingly.

Treatment of Minor and Superficial Wounds

- Expose the wound. Remove clothing by cutting away or gently undressing.
- Elevate the wound, if possible. This reduces blood pressure, swelling, and bleeding.
- Allow the wound to bleed a short while, but do not squeeze. Any squeezing may cause damage to the tissue.
- Do not disturb any blood clot that has already formed.
- Remove foreign objects and material that are easily removable.
- Take action to control bleeding by applying pressure to the wound.
- Cleanse the wound with mild soap and boiled water that has cooled. Use a rubbing stroke directed from the wound outward to minimize the chance of germs entering the wound.
- Apply an antiseptic dressing and bandage.
- Apply a splint, if the wound is near or on a joint, to keep the wound immobile.
- Watch for infection.

Treatment of Major and Complicated Wounds

Massive wounds require proper treatment to avoid complications at a later time. Pause to assess the situation fully since premature actions can aggravate the injury.

Most major wounds should be treated as follows:

- Restore respiration, if necessary.
- Stop hemorrhaging, if necessary.
- Treat for shock (See Section on Shock in this chapter.)
- Remove clothing from the wound area.
- Do not move the victim until you are sure that it is safe to do so. Moving the patient improperly might induce or intensify shock.
- Stop any bleeding by using the direct pressure technique.

(The exception is any injury where either brain, eye, or abdominal contents are exposed. If this is the case, then all and any pressure should be avoided and the wound merely covered with sterile gauze until proper treatment can be applied.)

- Take necessary steps to control severe bleeding. This may include using "pressure points" or even resorting to a tourniquet.
- Do not cleanse or use antiseptics when treating massive wounds.
- Give antibiotics to the patient.
- Do not give stimulants until the bleeding has been stopped, and then only if the patient is conscious.
- Obtain medical help immediately, if at all possible. (Obviously in the survival situation, you will have to judge type of medical treatment to be applied.)

FISHHOOK WOUNDS

Embedded fishhooks are one of the most commonly encountered accidents at sea. The seriousness of an embedded hook depends on the size of the hook, its location, and depth.

Treatment of Fishhook Wounds

- If the fishhook is in superficial skin, use a sterile razor blade and cut down through the skin to the shank of the hook and lift it out. Avoid cutting any visible blood vessels.
- Flood the wound with an antiseptic and then bandage.
- For a deeply *embedded fishhook,* push the hook through the skin until the barbed end comes through. Snip off the eye end of the shank (with wire cutters), then pull on the barbed end and ease out the shank (Fig. 10-4).
- Treat the wound with an antiseptic and apply a sterile bandage. (If a fishhook is in or near the eye, do not use an antiseptic.)

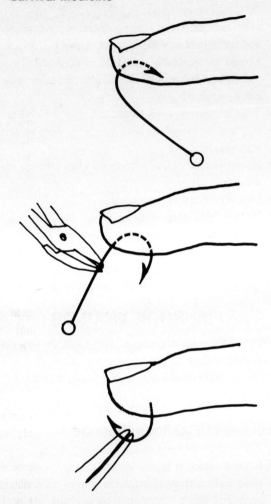

Fig. 10-4 Proper procedure for removing embedded fishhooks.

SHOCK

Shock results from an overtaxation of the nervous system, along with a drop in blood pressure, causing an inadequate blood flow to the brain and other vital organs of the body.

Shock varies in degree but is present, to some extent, in all injuries. Consequently, the understanding and recognition of it is important in any first aid treatment. The following section deals with injury-related shock, not electrical shock.

What Causes Shock?

Shock might follow any type of injury. The mere sight of blood can cause a person to become weak or nauseated, this is a mild form of shock usually followed by a quick recovery. Deep shock, however, may develop after severe injuries such as:

- Major crushing injuries
- Severe pain
- Fractures of the larger bones
- Great loss of blood

Shock might also result from such conditions as allergies, heat stroke, heart attack, infection, emotional stress, or poisoning (chemical or drug, and even extreme alcohol intoxication).

Types of Shock

Anaphalactic. Anaphalactic shock is an allergic shock from bee stings, portugese man-of-war jellyfish, or drug allergies (can be due to almost any drug).

Symptoms. Often just wheezing and a feeling of swelling in the mouth or throat. Sweating, weakness, dizziness, loss of consciousness, itchy rash, or hives might occur.

Neurogenic. The sight of blood, fear, or apprehension, causes neurogenic shock.

Symptoms. Victim might experience lightheadedness, faintness, or dizziness. Victim may be pale and sweaty.

Volume Depletion. Blood loss or severe dehydration causes volume depletion.

Symptoms. Symptoms are similar to other symptoms of shock, but the cause should be evident (bleeding, prolonged vomiting and/or diarrhea).

General Symptoms

- Clammy, pale, or cold skin. A bluish or ashen color may later develop.
- Rapid and weak heartbeat. (Pulse may be almost imperceptible.)
- Thirst or nausea.
- Shallow and rapid breathing.
- Victim may be restless, excited, apprehensive, hysterical, dizzy, or faint.
- An initially anxious expression may later change to a general dullness and a vacant, glassy stare.

Treatment

It is important to take immediate action. When treating for shock, your main objectives are to alleviate shock, shorten its duration, and prevent it from progressing or recurring.

- Eliminate the causes of shock by restoring breathing, controlling bleeding, and if possible, relieving any severe pain.
- Position the victim horizontally, lying down with the feet slightly higher (12 inches) than the head. This will increase the blood flow to the head. In the case of a head injury, reverse this procedure so that the head is higher than the rest of the body. (Do not elevate the legs or feet if a head or chest injury is present or if there is any difficulty in breathing.)
- Lay the victim on his side to allow for drainage from the nose and mouth if he is unconscious or has severe facial injuries.
- Cover the victim, if necessary, to maintain his normal body temperature.
- Loosen any constrictive clothing and reassure the person.
- Treat the basic injury.
- Administer appropriate drug, if available.

DROWNING

The treatment for drowning encompasses basic life support resuscitation techniques (Fig. 10-5).

If victim is not breathing, give mouth-to-mouth resuscitation, even if the victim is still in the water. Use a floatation device to support the victim's neck.

To enpty the stomach of a drowned victim once he is out of the water (on shore or in the raft), lay him in a face down position, lifting under the stomach with your hands to force the water out. The stomach of a drowned victim usually becomes distended because of the large amounts of water swallowed.

If the victim vomits, turn his head to the side and clear out his mouth. Continue resuscitation techniques until the victim is revived.

SEASICKNESS

Motion sickness on the ocean is called seasickness. Physiologically, it results from continuous "contradictory" messages and signals being transmitted to the brain. This causes a state of "confusion" as the brain attempts to sort out the conflicting signals. Your "inner ear" balance system (vestibular) is basically at odds with your "visual" reference system (the system providing information to the brain about one's position in relationship to the horizon), thus causing seasickness.

The following elements or combinations of elements may contribute to the conflicting information to the brain:

- The ocean's up and down motions
- The swaying and loss-of-balance sensation
- The eyes' automatic tendency to seek stationary references (horizon)
- The reaction of "position sensors" in your joints and tendons (especially the neck)

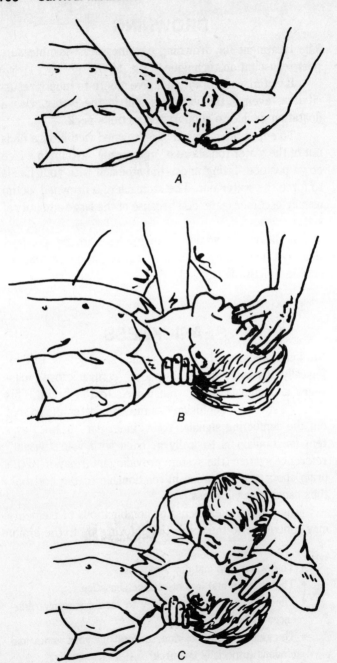

A

B

C

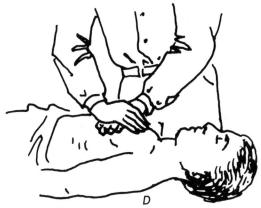

Fig. 10-5 The illustrations demonstrate the proper way to apply CPR techniques.

- Food, fatigue, illness, alcohol, drugs, and other individual factors may contribute.

In the survival environment, seasickness can be extremely dangerous. If vomiting occurs, vital body fluids will be lost and if water rations are low, it may mean the difference between surviving or death from dehydration. Repeated vomiting may prevent the taking of any orally administered medication. If this is the case, suppository application of medicine may be necessary.

Treatment

By nature of their absorbing qualities, small amounts of dry foods, crackers, bread, or similar foods may help to alleviate seasickness. Rest in a reclining position with the eyes closed, can aid the seasick person by minimizing the signals responsible for causing the seasickness.

BODILY ELIMINATION

A severe change of diet in the survival situation can cause chronic constipation. Some feel that this is beneficial in that any bowel movement requires body fluids and will result in the loss of precious water from the body.

Often a bowel movement will not occur for extended periods of time with no ill effects. Fresh water, if applied rectally via an enema, will aid in producing a bowel movement, but should only be administered if ample water is available. (Brackish water may be used.)

Urination should continue, although perhaps less frequently and in less quantity. When urine becomes dark in color or painful to pass, this is usually a symptom of dehydration, and is generally not harmful or unusual.

SWELLING

Swelling frequently occurs in the hands and feet. Gentle massage will help to alleviate the swelling. Joints tend to swell and become stiff and weak. Using and stretching joints several times a day will help to minimize the swelling.

BLISTERS AND BOILS

The buttocks and lower extremities may develop sores, boils, or blisters from continued exposure to wet conditions. Try to keep these areas dry, and change clothing frequently, if possible.

CRAMPS

Cramps in the limbs can occur from lack of use, loss of salt from the body, or excessive heat. Massage and knead the affected area.

DEATH

The confirmation and pronouncement of death is a medical decision that should be reserved for proper authorities when possible. Normally, attempts to resuscitate a victim should always continue until a physician arrives. In the survival situation, proper medical help may not be available, but nevertheless *all* attempts should be made to resuscitate a victim. This should be done not only for the sake of the victim, but also for the morale and spirit of the other crew members.

The will to live is the most valuable survival tool available to the castaway, and should be supported and reaffirmed at every instance. It is, however, necessary to be able to diagnose the termination of vital life signs to be fully confident that the person is deceased.

Death signs can be categorized in two basic classifications:

- Those that are apparent shortly after death (early signs)
- Those that are visible some hours or days after death has occurred; in most cases, death will be unmistakable when it occurs.

Suspecting Death

The complete absence of a heartbeat and lack of breathing for at least 20 minutes is an early sign of death. Remember that it is difficult to ascertain this without aid of medical equipment, such as a stethoscope.

Be complete in your diagnosis. Suspended animation (death trance) can result from electrical or injury-related shock. This condition produces an almost imperceptible heartbeat and pulse, a slowing down of other vital signs, and little or no trace of breathing.

When the heart stops beating, the pupils will begin to dilate within 45 seconds to 1 minute and will remain dilated, not reacting to light.

Using a mirror is the time-honored method of verification of death. By placing the mirror directly under the nose or mouth of the victim, any amount of breathing will be noticeable since the warm air of the breath will condense on the mirror.

If a mirror is not available, a light material, such as a cotton wisp can be used. If the surrounding air is calm enough, movement in the wisp can be noticed when it is held in front of the nose and mouth.

Later Signs

- A drop in body temperature. This is influenced by the amount of clothing the victim may be wearing, the air temperature, and the amount of time the victim has been dead.
- Appearance of the eyes. The transparency of the cornea turns into a milky or cloudy state and the surface becomes wrinkled.
- Rigor mortis. This is the stiffening of the muscles and general rigidity of the body. Although it is subject to variation, it usually appears within 2 to 8 hours after death and begins in the facial muscles, gradually extending to the legs. It lasts about 16 to 24 hours and will disappear in the same order as it appeared.
- Putrefecation. This is the rotting or decomposing of the body. Depending on the condition and temperature of the air, this process usually won't begin until one day after death and not until rigor mortis has disappeared. This is absolute verification of death.

Last Rites

The body of a dead person in the survival craft must be done away with for reasons of morale and health. A decomposing body could infect those around it.

All clothing and everything of any possible value should be taken off the corpse before discharging it into the sea. Any pertinent information should be recorded. The body may float for awhile, and if your raft is adrift the body may in fact follow the craft. If this happens, it can present emotional strain, but try to retain your perspective and composure.

The following prayer may be read upon commencement of a burial at sea:

"Almighty God, our Father, from whom we come and unto whom our spirits return: Thou hast been our dwelling place in all generations. Thou art our refuge and strength, a very present help in trouble. Grant us thy blessing in this hour, and enable us to put our trust in thee that our spirits may grow calm and our hearts be comforted. Lift our eyes beyond the shadows of the earth, and help us to see the light of eternity. So may we find grace and strength for this and every time of need. Amen."

11

Psychology
of Survival

THERE ARE AMPLE STORIES AND TEXTS AVAILable analyzing the facts and fiction of what it is like and what it takes to be a survivor. There are also detailed accounts written by actual survivors that focus specifically on the psychological aspects of the survival state. This chapter, while it is by no means a complete study in survival psychology, will familiarize you with the most common dilemmas and responses the castaway may experience.

THE SURVIVAL ATTITUDE

Man's ability to adapt, both physically and mentally, to adverse conditions will ultimately determine his outcome in a survival ordeal. History is full of examples of survival adaptation and fortitude that by "normal standards" would seem miraculous. History has also shown that physical prowess and strength are not necessarily prerequisites for survival. In survival conditions, mental attitudes play a far greater role in determining the outcome than many other factors.

Positive attitude is probably the most important factor in how to survive. A positive attitude is attainable even in the most bleak of circumstances. The continuous reaffirmation of a positive outlook is something that you can cultivate within yourself. It will ultimately contribute to your ability to adapt, and thus survive.

Endurance also comes from within and is an intrinsic part of the human will to live. Fortified by a positive attitude, endurance is the solid foundation for what must be present to withstand seemingly insurmountable odds.

People tend to limit themselves to do only what they think they can do. To survive you must accomplish tasks that are necessary for your survival even though they may seem beyond your limits. An open psychological attitude will help you overcome your own preconceived limits. It will also provide the psychological foundation necessary to see you through the duration of a survival ordeal.

INITIAL RESPONSE

An individual's response to catastrophe is difficult to anticipate. Man's primitive instincts are often reflected in his initial response to a threatening situation. The "every man for himself" attitude, for example, is typical of this type of basic instinct. It is usually triggered by a state of panic. Although this selfish survival instinct may seem abhorrent in action, it is nevertheless a natural aspect of human behavior. Remember also that, just as the "selfish" side of a person may surface in perilous conditions, so too may the valiant, sacrificing qualities of an individual.

The best approach to avoiding panic is to make sure that each crew member has been thoroughly drilled on emergency procedures beforehand, and has been given a specific role or job to carry out. This will direct the initial reactions away from panic and toward more constructive action.

IMMEDIATE POSITIVE ACTION

Before the shock of isolation and despair settles on the crew of a life raft, quick and decisive action is necessary. Positive action and the delegation of duties should begin immediately. For example, immediately begin salvaging any floating materials that may be of any possible use, assess the condition of the crew as to injuries, assess the condition of the raft, and inventory rations and supplies.

The important thing is to embark on a course of immediate positive activity. Purposeful action will enable you to deal most efficiently with your survival circumstances and will help ward off the initial paralyzing effects of shock and despair.

DEALING WITH ISOLATION

All castaways must deal with the isolation and loneliness inherent in their situation. Along with isolation comes fear and uncertainty. The constant belief and reaffirmation that you will survive is essential in helping to control fear. The key to dealing with isolation is to establish order and purpose in a situation that may otherwise seem chaotic and overwhelming.

Establish routines and make sure everyone adheres to them. This will create order and stability. Include every person in these routines and duties, even if (as in the case of injured crew members) this means assigning trivial tasks. This allows each crew member to feel that he is contributing to the overall welfare of the group, and to feel useful and purposeful. It also ensures that certain necessary duties are accomplished and that there is a minimum of wasted or duplicated efforts.

It is also important to establish goals to provide the desperate castaway with a purpose for his actions. Whether they are long-term or short-term goals (such as reaching a shipping lane or catching dinner), goals will help divert the castaway's mind from feelings of despair and isolation. Establishing a realistic goal that is supported by routines will not only provide the castaway with something to look forward to, but will also help keep his mind focused in a positive direction.

EMOTIONAL STATES

* The isolated castaway is vulnerable to experiencing loneliness, boredom, depression, anxiety, resignation, and despair, sometimes at severe levels. Any one of these conditions at an extreme level can represent a significant threat to the castaway by displacing purposeful actions or causing irrational behavior. The potentially detrimental effects of any one, or a combination of these emotional states can be lessened by constant affirmative action and by keeping the mind occupied.

In a group situation, it is important to pursue actions that support and bolster the morale of the entire group. The depressed mind is capable of doing anything. A person who throws himself overboard in an apparent attempt to drown himself might be demonstrating a need. By saving this person you will demonstrate to the others that life is important and that there is still hope left in the situation. Patience, encouragement, reassurance, and support will do more to develop the confidence of a distraught crew member than urgent demands or desperate appeals of logic.

The castaway is likely to suffer low emotional states following thwarted expectations, such as the sighting of a potential rescue ship that fails to see him. To be emotionally prepared for the disappointment of being "passed by," the castaway must not pin all of his hopes on a chance rescue, but instead must continue to adhere to his daily routines and long-term goals. With today's widespread use of sophisticated navigational aids and automatic pilots on ships and planes, it is easy to see how highly automated vessels could pass by a small life raft, even at very close range. In one documented case in which the castaways were adrift for 117 days, they sighted six ships before they were finally rescued by a seventh.

Mirages are a common phenomenon, both on land and at sea, and can be very confusing and disorienting. The castaway must also be on guard for the disappointment and "let down" that can result from mistaking a mirage for a landfall or a rescue ship. Mirages can change appearance and height while being viewed, and can also shimmer or disappear. Heat, light, and refraction all combine to give the false appearance of such images as land, ships, or even (when combined with exhaustion and dehydration) outright hallucinations. Experiencing mirages at sea does not necessarily mean that the castaway is suffering from delusions.

Affirmative actions, positive attitudes, and long-range goals cannot be over emphasized in a survival situation. Dangerous and paralyzing emotional states arising from feelings of desperation and hopelessness can be as grave a threat to the castaway as the lack of food or water. The degree to which a survivor is effective in carrying out the vital tasks of obtaining food and water will be influenced by his emotional state of health.

DIRECTED ACTIVITY

An important part of daily existence will be finding constructive ways to pass time. This can help to displace negative emotions that could inhibit your ability to function. A purposefully occupied mind is less likely to indulge in such counterproductive feelings as pity and despair.

Passing time in the group situation can consist of playing games, learning skills, tying knots, or storytelling. Relating past experiences to each other or detailing descriptions of future plans or even fantasizing daydreams aloud can also be effective. All of these can provide a positive way to pass time.

Prayer, self-hypnosis, and meditation can also provide support and activity to the crew. This type of quiet, directed mental activity is far better than undirected listless-ness. It is also superior to physical activities that often require exertion and burn up precious calories the body may need. Use physical energy primarily for food and water gathering activities.

PRIORITY SURVIVAL

As rations are depleted during the course of the survival period, there may come a point where the amount of supplies available is not sufficient to allow every crew member to remain coherent. It may be necessary at this point to choose one person, the strongest, to be given more rations. The purpose behind this course of action is to actually increase the chance for the entire group to survive. It allows for at least one person to remain alert enough to recognize and signal a passing vessel, gather food, or to effect a landfall. Although this course of action may run counter to the natural survival instinct of "every man for himself," it is important to realize that it may ultimately serve the best interests of the group. The important goal is survival.

APPENDIX

Abandon Ship Bag Checklist

Abandon Ship Bag

CHECKLIST

Supply your abandon ship bag with the equipment necessary to meet your cruising requirements and personal preferences. This list is only a suggestion.

- ☐ 3 HANDHELD RED PARACHUTE FLARES
- ☐ 3 HANDHELD RED FLARES
- ☐ 2 HANDHELD ORANGE SMOKE SIGNALS
- ☐ 1 CLASS B (MANUAL) EPIRB
- ☐ 1 HANDHELD VHF RADIO
- ☐ 1 WATERTIGHT BAG FOR VHF
- ☐ 1 SIGNAL MIRROR
- ☐ 1 WHISTLE OR HORN
- ☐ 1 AM-FM RADIO WITH SPARE BATTERIES
- ☐ 2 WATERPROOF FLASHLIGHTS WITH SPARE BATTERIES
- ☐ 12 CYALUME CHEMICAL LIGHTSTICKS
- ☐ 1 HANDBEARING COMPASS
- ☐ 1 WATERPROOF WATCH WITH SWEEPHAND
- ☐ 1 LIFERAFT PATCH KIT
- ☐ 1 SPARE RAFT PUMP
- ☐ 1 SEA ANCHOR
- ☐ 2 CIGARETTE LIGHTERS
- ☐ 1 BOX ZIP-LOCK TYPE BAGS

FISHING
- ☐ 1 FISH KNIFE
- ☐ 1 SPEAR GUN WITH EXTRA TIPS
- ☐ 12 FISHHOOKS OF VARYING SIZES
- ☐ 1 SPOOL 80 POUND-TEST LINE
- ☐ 20 FEET WIRE LEADER
- ☐ 1 WIRE SAW

FOOD
- ☐ 1 WATERMAKER
- ☐ 1 GALLON FOLDABLE JUG
- ☐ 1 VERKADE HIGH-ENERGY FOOD RATIONS AND OTHER FOOD BY PREFERENCE
- ☐ 1 CAN OPENER
- ☐ 1 CONTAINER OF HONEY IN UNBREAKABLE JAR
- ☐ 1 GRADUATED DRINKING CUP
- ☐ 30 WATER PACKETS

PERSONAL
- ☐ 1 SET POLYPROPYLENE UNDERWEAR
- ☐ 1 TOOTHBRUSH
- ☐ 1 LONG SLEEVED SHIRT
- ☐ PHOTOCOPY OF PASSPORT
- ☐ $50 CASH
- ☐ DUPLICATE CREDIT CARDS
- ☐ SUNGLASSES
- ☐ WATERLESS CLEANSING TOWELS
- ☐ 1 THERMAL BLANKET

MEDICAL
- ☐ SEASICKNESS PILLS
- ☐ SUNBURN CREAM
- ☐ VASELINE
- ☐ MULTIVITAMINS
- ☐ BATHROOM TISSUE
- ☐ POCKET NOTEBOOKS
- ☐ PENCILS
- ☐ FIRST AID KIT AND MANUAL
- ☐ REEDS ALMANAC

©1987 SURVIVAL TECHNOLOGIES GROUP   11600 NINTH STREET NORTH, ST. PETERSBURG, FL 33702-1098

(Courtesy Survival Technologies Group.)

Index

(Note: Emergency information is in bold face type for quickest reference.)